THE ETHICS
OF
G. E. MOORE
AND
DAVID HUME:

The *Treatise* as a Response
to Moore's
Refutation of Ethical Naturalism

Richard J. Soghoian

University Press
of America™

Library of Congress Catalog Card Number: 79-88306

ACKNOWLEDGEMENT

This is my first opportunity to acknowledge in writing the debt I owe to Professor Charles Frankel, for his deep humanity as a teacher, wisdom as a philosopher, and patience as a critic and mentor of this work in its formative stages as a Ph.D. dissertation at Columbia University.

I wish also to express my appreciation to my parents, whose faith in learning was to my great benefit passed on to me. To them I dedicate this work.

INTRODUCTION

G. E. Moore is rightly associated in our century as the founder and chief defender of the claim that most ethical theories are guilty of a fundamental mistake. This negative claim has been expressed in many ways, with varying degrees of subtlety, but it generally flourishes under the form and name given to it by Moore in his *Principia Ethica,* "the naturalistic fallacy." My purpose in writing this book is to evaluate a somewhat restricted aspect of this general claim, that part of it which is directed against "naturalistic ethical theories," in a way which is historically as well as philosophically significant. If most, or even some, naturalistic ethical theories commit a fundamental mistake, it is important to know and to exhibit this—in order to avoid such a mistake in the future. But if no such mistake has been committed, then it is equally important to know this—in oder, at least, to correct a far-reaching historical error.

The importance of this question remains, however, for the most part a philosophical one. It is not Moore as a writer on ethics that interests me, but the fundamental nature of ethics in so far as it is dealt with by Moore. Moore's contribution to the question, which is considerable in its influence, is fundamental to any understanding of the development of ethical theory in this century. My concern nevertheless is not so much to improve our historical know-

1

ledge as to improve our ethical thinking. False historical interpretation is generally representative of deeper errors, of deeper substantive issues that ought to be our main concern. We interpret with the same tools and with the same intentions as those we build with. Indeed, Moore's negative views have not only proved to be the most influential aspect of his ethical theory, but have provided the force behind his general approach to ethics as well. Some thinkers have gone so far as to accept Moore's negative position as the basic enterprise of ethical theory itself. A. J. Ayer underlines this point by frankly and confidently showing that he arrives at his theory entirely by eliminating all alternatives through a form of the "naturalistic fallacy argument."[1] Consequently, if it turns out that Moore fails in one direction, in his negative, historical claims, then we should raise questions in the other. And if he fails in the other direction, in his positive, substantive theory, then we ought to question his general approach to the subject.

It is surprising to me that critics of Moore's ethical theory, from Frankena's famous essay, "The Naturalistic Fallacy," to the present, have neglected to do so. Criticism of Moore has been largely confined to questions of internal consistency and strength.[2] One result of this detailed and thorough, but restricted criticism, has been to leave the student of philosophy with the impression that the general approach, the questions posed and the directions taken by Moore are essentially correct, and that only his *answers* to these are incorrect. And, indeed, Moore himself rejects later in his career many of the essential particulars of his "naturalistic fallacy argument" without diminishing substantially his own or the general acceptance of his approach to ethical enquiry.[3] In this respect also a sort of tradition in ethical enquiry arose after Moore, following not so much the details of his argument, as the broad approach. I mean by a tradition here a common set of assumptions and attitudes, a general agreement as to the main problems, an identifiable way, in short, of going about ethical enquiry. Who would deny, for instance, that the magnificent opening words of the Preface to *Principia Ethica* are just as appropriate to Ross or Ayer or Stevenson or Hare, to name only a few important figures? Moore says, "it appears to me that in Ethics, as in all other philosophical studies, the difficulties and disagreements, of which its history is full, are mainly due to a very simple cause: namely to the attempt to answer questions, without first discovering precisely *what* question it is which you desire to answer."[4] Here is the appealing assumption that "if only this attempt were made, many of the most glaring difficulties and disagreements in philosophy would disappear."[5] Here also is the assumption that there is a *Real* question in ethics, and with it, its counterpart (for those who would accept the former) that there is also a *Real* mistake. Perhaps, but the point I am trying to emphasize here is that the force and significance of Moore's ethics stem more from his general approach than from any single argument or set of arguments. Consequently, to evaluate his negative, historical claim, it is not enough to isolate and detail his arguments, but to seek more comprehensive questions, questions which could be posed with equal fairness to "previous ethical theories" as well as to Moore's own theory. It seems to me that only in this way can we properly focus our

2

historical perspective, if it turns out, of course, that this is what is needed.

I have chosen what I believe to be a natural and direct approach to these issues. I selected Hume as the most sophisticated and substantive of ethical "naturalists" and developed a form of dialogue between him and Moore. I begin by trying to determine quite clearly how Moore views ethical enquiry, exhibiting the themes and assumptions which support and are implied by his contentions. Ultimately, I pose to both Moore and Hume the same questions, attempting to determine on which points dialogue is possible and on which points misunderstanding has led to cross-purposes.[6]

In the Preface to *Principia Ethica*, for example, Moore states his main intention: "I have tried in this book to distinguish clearly two kinds of questions, which moral philosophers have always professed to answer, but which. . . they have almost always confused both with one another and with other questions." These are, "What kind of things ought to exist for their own sakes?" and "What kind of actions ought we to perform?"[7] This is a rather extraordinary indictment. Could it be justified? Did Hume, as an example, ever confuse these questions? Or, did he perhaps neglect the former and consequently, as Moore suggests, at the cost of ever answering the latter? Moore's position appears to become more questionable when he goes on to say that these two questions are preliminary to a "second most important result: namely, what is the nature of the evidence, by which alone any ethical proposition can be proved or disproved, confirmed or rendered doubtful."[8] For the question here is not whether Hume ever confused these issues, but whether he ever thought that knowing what kind of things ought to exist for their own sakes is preliminary to answering the question, which ethical propositions are susceptible to proof and which are not. And though Hume, of course, is also centrally concerned with the justification and warranty of our ethical judgments, there is the further interesting question whether he ever sees a possible solution in terms of propositions and their evidential bases.

Moreover, the crucial debate in contemporary ethics concerning the relationship between fact and value arises in perhaps its clearest form in a dialogue between Hume and Moore. The central claim of *Principia Ethica* is the claim that the moral quality of goodness is simple, indefinable, and unanalyzable. It is this claim which supports the two principle themes of that book, the broad negative one that there is a fundamental mistake "to be met with in almost every book on Ethics,"[9] and the positive one that in the case of intrinsic moral judgments "no relevant evidence whatever can be adduced: from no other truth, except themselves alone, can it be inferred that they are either true or false."[10] Ethics is, according to Moore, autonomous in the strictest formal sense, and any attempt to relate it to, or make it dependent upon, something else involves a fallacy. Moore's main concern in Chapter I of *Principia Ethica* is the "proof" of such a fallacy in the case of the moral quality "good" and the rejection of any attempt to interpret or reduce this moral quality to anything else, either metaphysical or natural. The argument in Chapter I concerning "good" is a rejection, then, in specialized form of the general view that the nature of the world *does* have a bearing on ethical truths. To put the matter in

3

contemporary terminology, statements of value are logically distinct from statements of fact, and any attempt to deduce or infer a statement of value from statements of fact involves what Moore calls "the naturalistic fallacy."

It is obvious that such a prohibition strikes at the heart of Hume's moral theory. In Hume's theory, as in any moral theory which falls under the broad concept of "naturalism," moral predicates refer to empirical properties, or "impressions" in Hume's terminology. It follows that moral judgments are factual judgments and, like all such judgments, in some sense confirmable. It is reasonable, then, to expect Hume to maintain that moral judgments are inferable from other factual judgments, presumably judgments about the impressions and the circumstances under which they appear. And if this is the case, Hume is clearly in direct opposition to Moore. Indeed, it is on the issue of the inferability of value from fact or the nature of the dichotomy between them that the contemporary critique of naturalism in ethics is centered.

In addition to the substantive issue of the relationship between fact and value, a significant historical question arises as well. It is often contended that the prohibition against inferring value from fact, or an "ought" from an "is," comes from a famous passage in Hume's *Treatise*. In other words, some would argue that Hume himself denies the validity of such inferences, so that even if Moore's understanding of such a proscription is erroneous, nevertheless, in Hume's mind such a proscription exists. This is the very position in which we find Frankena in his essay, "The Naturalistic Fallacy." Although the essay involves a detailed attempt to refute the "naturalistic fallacy," i. e. Moore's defense of non-inferability, Frankena nevertheless maintains that "Hume's point is that ethical conclusions cannot be drawn validly from premises which are non-ethical."[11] This identification of the "naturalistic fallacy" with the supposed Is-Ought proscription of the *Treatise* generates one of the most paradoxical and yet ignored questions in historical interpretation: Why, if the "naturalistic fallacy" is identical with Hume's Is-Ought contention, does Hume expound a proscription which his own philosophical position so clearly violates? Could Hume, perhaps the subtlest of modern thinkers, be guilty of such an obvious inconsistency? It seems hardly possible that this could be the case, yet the question remains and demands an answer.

One might ask why such an indirect road is needed to prove that "naturalistic ethical theories" are not guilty of a fundamental fallacy. If such theories are supposedly guilty of reducing ethical value to factual condition, why not simply demonstrate that value is inferable from fact and therefore that there is no strict or logical distinction between the two areas? Why not give, in other words, an independent proof of the inferability of "ought" from "is"?[12]

There are a number of good reasons for choosing to approach the issue through an analysis of Moore's and Hume's ethical theories. The non-inferability of "ought" from "is" is almost unanimously identified both with Moore's "naturalistic fallacy" and Hume's Is-Ought statement. So that an evaluation of both positions will not only introduce us to the fundamental issue, but will give us a better understanding of the origins of this contention in contemporary ethics. Moreover, the interesting historical question why Hume propounds a

4

proscription which his own ethical position appears to violate would otherwise remain unanswered. And this question is not only important from the point of view of historical fact, but an answer to it will no doubt shed further light on the structure of contemporary ethical theory, a structure which is used both to interpret as well as to build. And lastly, even if an independent proof could be given for inferability, it would still remain an open question whether "naturalistic ethical theories" successfully accomplish this task. By carrying on a sort of dialogue-by-issue between the positions of Moore and Hume in respect to the contemporary critique of ethical naturalism, we can, I believe, bring into historical as well as theoretical focus the fundamental issues of contemporary ethical theory itself.

There is, then, a whole family of questions concerning Moore's interpretation of traditional ethical theories, especially those called "naturalistic," and his own view of the nature and purpose of ethical enquiry. And it is this family of questions which points to some significant sense in which the thinking, attitudes, and assumptions, which underlie Moore's position in ethics, are also the guiding forces behind his questionable historical judgments. There appears to be, in short, a parallel of misinterpretation, on the one hand, and theory, on the other, both receiving their force and vitality from a number of common sources in Moore's *Principia Ethica*.

[1] Alfred Jules Ayer, *Language, Truth, and Logic,* New York, Dover Publications, Inc., n.d., Chapter IV, cf. p. 104.

[2] There are at least two important exceptions to this: Everett Hall, "The 'Proof' of Utility in Bentham and Mill", in Categorical Analysis, ed. by E. M. Adams, Chapel Hill, The University of North Carolina Press, 1964. A. W. Levi, "The Trouble with Ethics: Values, Method, and the Search for Moral Norms," *Mind,* vol. 70, 1961.

[3] Moore's most comprehensive reassessment of his original position in *Principia Ethica* is to be found in his "A Reply to My Critics" in *The Philosophy of G. E. Moore,* ed. by Paul Arthur Schilpp, New York, Tudor Publishing Company, 1952, p. 14. But apparently Moore reconsidered some important aspects of *Principia* as early as the second edition of that work in a yet unpublished and unfinished draft of a proposed new preface. See C. Lewy's essay, "G. E. Moore on the Naturalistic Fallacy", *The Proceedings of the British Academy,* Vol. L, 1964, Oxford University Press.

[4] G. E. Moore, *Principia Ethica,* Cambridge, University Press, 1962, p. vii.

[5] *Ibid.,* p. vii.

[6] Everett Hall's essay, "The 'Proof' of Utility in Bentham and Mill," (see note 2) admirably develops in respect to Benthan and Mill the sort of critical dialogue with Moore's negative views that I have in mind here. Professor Hall, however, limits his essay to the broad methodological misunderstandings between these men, as opposed to the more substantive issues, which Hume's theory, I feel, is better suited to represent.

[7] *Principia,* pp. vii-viii.

[8] *Ibid.,* p. viii.

[9] *Ibid.,* p. 14.

[10] *Ibid.,* p. viii.

[11] W. Frankena, "The Naturalistic Fallacy," in *Readings in Ethical Theory,* ed. by W. Sellars and J. Hospers, New York, Appleton-Century-Crofts, 1952, p.

[12] A significant attempt to do so is made by John Searle in his essay, "How to Derive 'Ought' From 'Is'," *Philosophical Review,* Vol. 73, 1964, pp. 43-58.

CHAPTER ONE

The central claim of *Principia Ethica* is the claim that the moral quality of goodness is simple, indefinable, and unanalyzable. It is this claim which supports the two principal themes of that book, the broad negative one that there is a fundamental mistake "to be met with in almost every book on Ethics,"[1] and the positive one that in the case of intrinsic moral judgments "no relevant evidence whatever can be adduced: from no other truth, except themselves alone, can it be inferred that they are either true or false."[2] This work is an attempt to evaluate these general claims, primarily as they bear on Hume's ethical theory and generate thereby a number of critical issues.

There are two levels or points of view from which we can consider this relationship. There is the broad view of Hume as "representative of naturalism" and Moore as "critic of naturalism:" on the one hand, the position that, though there is an obvious distinction between moral experience and other types of experience, each draws upon the other, both in terms of content as well as meaning, while on the other hand, the position that there is a *logical* distinction to be drawn between ethics and all other realms. And secondly, there is the more restricted view detailing the specific issues on which Hume and Moore build their theories and on which they frequently disagree. The question con-

7

cerning the nature and role of definition is such an issue. This issue is not necessarily involved in the broad controversy of "naturalism" versus "non-naturalism." There is no type of definition which is peculiar to one or the other of these two positions, so that we could survey and possibly settle the controversy from the point of view of the question of definition. Yet the manner in which Moore treats this question has a definite and crucial bearing on his ultimate ethical position. It is for this reason that we should begin by determining Moore's position on the nature and role of definition, its relationship to his general argument in ethics, and its significance for Hume's ethical position. It is only by exhibiting first of all the details of Moore's theoretical framework, that we can hope to evaluate successfully his challenge to "naturalistic ethical theories" and ultimately to develop a dialogue concerning the general principles of morality.

The Major Themes of Principia Ethica

In his review of Brentano's *The Origin of the Knowledge of Right and Wrong,* Moore gives clear expression to the two major themes of *Principia Ethica,* published that same year:

> ... all truths of the form "This is good in itself" are logically independent of any truth about what exists. No ethical proposition of this form is such that, if a certain thing exists, it is true, whereas, if that thing does not exist, it is false. All such ethical truths are true, *whatever the nature of the world may be.*[3]

Ethics (in its primary sense) is, according to Moore, autonomous in the strictest formal sense, and any attempt to relate it to, or make it dependent upon, something else is a fallacy. Moore's main concern in Chapter I of *Principia Ethica* is the "proof" of such a fallacy in the case of the moral quality "good" and the rejection of any attempt to interpret or reduce this moral quality to anything else, either metaphysical or natural. The argument in Chapter I concerning "good" is a rejection, then, in specialized form of the general view that the nature of the world *does* have a bearing on ethical truths, both in their primary as well as their secondary senses. But so much for the implications of the fallacy; these should naturally gain clarity and significance in the course of our discussion of the preliminary issues of Moore's first chapter. Our present concern is with the nature of the fallacy and the argument which supports it.

In respect to metaphysical interpretations, where "good" is identified with objects "inferred to exist in a supersensible world,"[4] the fallacy is in failing to perceive "that any truth which asserts 'This is good in itself' is quite unique in kind—that it cannot be reduced to any assertion about reality, and therefore must remain unaffected by any conclusions we may reach about the nature of reality."[5] In respect to naturalistic interpretations, where "good" is identified with objects "of which the existence is admittedly an object of experience,"[6] the fallacy consists in "substituting for 'good' some one property of a natural object or a collection of natural objects; and in thus replacing Ethics by some one of the natural sciences."[7] Both metaphysical and naturalistic ethical theories are guilty of the general fallacy of reducing Ethics to what is not Ethics, of identifying "good" with what it is not. But Moore nevertheless believes that naturalistic ethical theories are more clearly guilty of such a false identification than other sorts of ethical theories and therefore more clearly to be rejected. He says, referring to the results of Chapter I,

> So much, then, for the first step in our ethical method, the step which established that good is good and nothing else whatever, and that Naturalism was a fallacy.[8]

If "good" is simple and indefinable, any argument based on a definition of goodness must be unsound, and the plausibility of any suggested definition must lie in confusing the simple quality of goodness with some other quality. What could lead one to attempt to define goodness and consequently to confuse goodness with that something else, i.e. to commit the naturalistic fallacy? Moore believes,

> We are, therefore, justified in concluding that the attempt to define good is chiefly due to want of clearness as to the possible nature of definition.[9]

Accordingly, let us turn to what Moore has to say about definition and attempt to see if it explains, in particular, Hume's "mistaken" attempt to define goodness and, more generally, perhaps, why "Naturalism was a fallacy."

Moore's Theory of Definition

Moore's view of definition is on the face of it quite straightforward and clear. He seems to be saying that simple terms or parts are the ultimate unanalyzable building blocks of complex terms or wholes and that definition is the statement of those simple terms or parts which compose a given whole. Meaning, then, is determined in reference to these "simples," either (as in the case of definition) by enumeration or (as in the case of experience) by direct perception. That the meaning of something is identical to the nature of its constitution viewed from the point of view of its simplest parts or terms is not directly stated in *Principia Ethica*, yet is is clearly implied by a number of Moore's statements. He says, in summary of the conclusions of Chapter I,

> It results from the conclusions of Chapter I, that all ethical questions fall under one or other of three classes. The first class contains one question—the question What is the nature of that peculiar predicate, the relation of which to other things constitutes the object of all other ethical investigations? or, in other words, What is *meant* by good? This first question I have already attempted to answer. The peculiar predicate, by reference to which the sphere of Ethics must be defined, is simple, unanalyzable, indefinable."[10]

In other words, to question the *meaning* of something is to question the nature of that thing, and to question something's *nature* is to investigate its part-whole relationships. Since "good" has no parts and definition is the statement of the parts that compose a given whole, then "good" has no *definitional* meaning; one can say no more about its nature and consequently its meaning, than it is simple, unanalyzable, and indefinable. Moore says,

> . . . if I am asked 'What is good?' my answer is that good is good, and that is the end of the matter. Or if I am asked 'How is good to be defined?' my answer is that it cannot be defined, and that is all

I have to say about it.[11]

The following related points, then, seem to constitute Moore's general view of definition: a) that definition is enumeration of the simple parts that compose a given whole and that consequently only complexes can be defined and b) that the *real* meaning and *real* nature of a thing are identical to one another and that consequently only those things whose natures can be given, i.e. analyzed, in terms of their parts, can also be given a verbal meaning. In short, on the above view, the notions of simplicity, unanalyzability, indefinability, and meaning function on the same common denominator. If one shows that something is simple and unanalyzable, one shows at the same time that it is indefinable and without statable meaning. And if one shows that something is indefinable, that its meaning cannot be stated, one shows that that something has a simple nature, that is is unanalyzable.

This seems to be Moore's general position on the nature and role of definition. It is the position, moreover, which provides the backbone for the main argument in Chapter I of *Principia Ethica,* though Moore surprisingly treats the question of defintion there in an off-hand and unhelpfully brief manner. The question of definition, however, is quite complex, and Moore's off-hand treatment of it tends to obscure rather than clarify its relationship to the argument as a whole. There is an understandable reluctance, therefore, to regard the question of definition as primary. In this respect, Mary Warnock concludes,

> I do not think one should waste very much time on Moore's eccentric treatment of the word 'defintion'. For one thing, the concept of definition is itself very vague, and it is not clear that anything very important would come of laying down the different ways in which things may or may not be defined. Furthermore, if we drop the word 'definition'. . . nothing much will be lost.[12]

But perhaps much will be lost. If, as Professor Warnock says, the question of definition is quite complex, then it may be quite important to determine exactly why Moore mistakenly regards the question as clear and straightforward. Indeed, previous ethical theories are extraordinarily varied and complex, yet Moore believes that all of them are doing essentially the same thing and commit essentially the same mistake! Virtually the whole of moral experience and discussion is evidence for the complexity and relativity of goodness—yet Moore believes that goodness is a simple and constant something! And if it is mistaken thinking that leads him to over-simplify and misunderstand the question of definition, it may well be the *same* sort of mistaken thinking that leads him to over-simplify his interpretation of previous ethical theories and the nature of goodness.

Perhaps the most practical way of forming a complete picture of Moore's view of definition is to look closely at the important passages immediately preceding his introduction of the "naturalistic fallacy" claim and to unravel the various threads of argument there. These should lead us to the key points in Chapter I which complete his view of definition and the critical claims which rest upon it.

The Nature of the Moral Property or Quality "Good"

In Chapter I, Moore refers to goodness equally as a "quality," "notion," "object," "thing," "term," "property," "idea," and "part." Moreover, he neither justifies the interchangeability of these terms nor suggests a preference for one or the other of them. Indeed, he nowhere even intimates that there might be relevant differences between some of them.[13] Consequently, the question immediately arises as to what general sort of thing Moore is referring to by the term "good." Without this information, the reader is substantially handicapped while trying to relate the various arguments, examples, and analogies in Chapter I. There is, for example, an analogy of "good" with "yellow," which emphasizes the term "quality."[14] There is the "open question argument," which employs the terms "unique object" and "unique property."[15] And there is a "horse" example, which employs the terms "quality," "property," and "part."[16] Accordingly, we ought to consider the possible differences between these terms and the various difficulties for Moore's general argument that any differences might create.

Moore's use of various terms in referring to goodness is considered confusing but unimportant by Mary Warnock. She says,

> There is a certain amount of confusion here and elsewhere in the discussion, about whether we are supposed to be discussing a word or some object denoted by a word, such as a property; but this confusion is not very important.[17]

Professor Warnock's position here is quite in agreement with her view that Moore's theory of definition is unimportant, as well, to the argument as a whole. Nevertheless, it is only if we do recognize the central importance of Moore's theory of definition, that we can recognize the crucial differences that appear to result from the interchange of these terms.

In the opening passages of Section 10, where Moore introduces the analogy of "good" with the quality "yellow," he suggests that goodness is also a quality and that it is in this sense of goodness that it is indefinable and simple. He says,

> 'Good,' then, if we mean by it that quality which we assert to belong to a thing, when we say that the thing is good, is incapable of any definition, in the most important sense of that word. The most important sense of 'definition' is that in which a definition states what are the parts which invariably compose a certain whole; and in this sense 'good' has no definition because it is simple and has no parts.[18]

There are a number of peculiarities in this passage which raise questions as to the significance and validity of the "most important sense of definition." Moore seems to be presenting here an argument in summary form for the indefinability of "good." It appears to run as follows:

(1) Definition in its most important sense is the statement of those parts which invariably compose a given whole.

(2) "Good is simple and has no parts.

(3) .. "Good" is indefinable.

11

Now, this certainly is no *proof* that "good" is indefinable. If something has no parts, then it is both simple and indefinable—by definition—on Moore's position. In order to prove that something which has no parts is indefinable, one would have to prove independently that definition in its most important sense is the enumeration of those parts which invariably compose a given whole.

However, perhaps Moore is not arguing here, but only explaining what is involved in the view that "good" is a simple quality. This would explain the real peculiarity in the above passage. Moore begins by saying that "good" is a quality. He implies by this that there are in fact complex and simple qualities in his sense of those terms, viz. respectively as having and as not having *parts*. But "qualities," I naturally assume, have no parts. I am not sure, at least, what sense, if any, one could make of the notion, "part of a quality." The only example of an analysis of a quality in Chapter I, other than of goodness, itself, is Moore's analysis of the quality "yellow." But, since "yellow" turns out *not* to have "parts," the question remains whether there are qualities which *do* not have "parts," i.e. whether Moore's view of analysis is at all relevant to the proper analysis and understanding of qualities.

Consequently, it is misleading to follow the assumption that goodness is a quality with what can easily be mistaken for an argument for the indefinability of goodness. At best, Moore's position here is merely verbal and, like all such positions, provides no basis for substantive conclusions. If we are to assume that goodness is a quality, then the preliminary issue obviously is not whether goodness is simple and indefinable, but whether there are simple and complex qualities in virtue of their having or not having parts—or, what amounts to the same question, whether Moore's theory of definition is indeed the most important and relevant sense of definition in ethics.

Not only, then, does Moore's position on the question of definition bear directly on the immediate issues in Chapter I, but clearly has important implications for ethical theory. For if his were the primary sense of definition, the sense of definition which any serious ethical theory must employ, then those theories which Moore labels "naturalistic ethical theories" would be eliminated by definition—on Moore's theory of definition. Naturalistic ethical theories are characterized by Moore as those theories which identify moral value with objects "of which the existence is admittedly an object of experience."[19] Consequently, if we exclude the possibility of ever giving significant definitions of any and all qualities, we would cut off so-called "naturalistic ethical theories" from their source and content. To identify and define (in some sense of definition) those "qualities" in experience which give content and meaning to our moral judgments and actions is the necessary task of any ethical theory which claims to be practical and claims to say something *about the world*.

In this respect, W. Frankena has raised the general question whether Moore is correct as to the purpose of definition in ethics. Frankena believes that Moore has no right to prejudge the role of definition in ethics as a preliminary necessity to theorizing.[20] I quite agree, but my point here is that it is not the necessity of definition as a preliminary step, but Moore's theory of definition which prejudges the case against naturalism in ethics. And it is quite understandable that Moore, who believes that

> ... any truth which asserts 'This is good in itself' is quite unique in kind—that it cannot be reduced to any assertion about reality, and therefore must remain unaffected by any conclusions we may reach about the nature of reality.[21]

should employ a sense of definition which prejudges the case against naturalism in ethics.

Furthermore, the naturalistic fallacy would indeed be an obvious fallacy, even more obvious and simple than Moore repeatedly suggests. It would be the fallacy of attempting to define, by the enumeration of the simple parts which compose it, something which admittedly has no parts. It would be quite unreasonable to accept this as the most common mistake committed by previous ethical philosophers. It is much more reasonable to assume (if we must) that previous ethical philosophers either employ some sense of definition other than Moore's or that they, like Moore, think it correct not to define goodness. The point, in short, is that if goodness is a *quality,* then it is difficult to see what justification Moore has for the view that "The most important sense of 'definition' is that in which a definition states what are the parts which invariably compose a certain whole."[22] Indeed, the real difficulty is in trying to understand why Moore does not recognize the obvious implication of this view of goodness, namely, the implication that definition in his sense is simply *not relevant* to ethics.

Thus, if we approach the question whether or not goodness is simple, unanalyzable, and indefinable, from the point of view of its being a quality, we find ourselves faced with the question whether definition in its most important sense is the enumeration of those "ultimate terms"[23] which invariably compose a given whole. That Moore either fails to recognize the real issue here or ignores it for the purposes of his argument, may be disclosed by continuing the passage that we have been discussing. Moore wants us to believe that the issue is whether "good" is a simple something, an "ultimate term" or "simplest part." He wants us to believe that the plausibility of his view is contingent on the plausibility that "good" is a simple something, and not on his theory of definition. He says,

> "Good" is one of those innumerable objects of thought which are themselves incapable of definition, because they are the ultimate terms by reference to which whatever is capable of definition must be defined. That there must be an indefinite number of such terms is obvious, on reflection; since we cannot define anything except by an analysis, which, when carried as far as it will go, refers us to something, which is simply different from anything else, and which by that ultimate difference explains the peculiarity of the whole which we are defining: for every whole contains some parts which are common to other wholes also.[24]

A number of complicated threads come together here. First, Moore refers to "good" equally as "ultimate term," "quality," "parts which are common to other wholes," and "ultimate difference." If we add to this list three terms employed by Moore earlier in Chapter I and subsequently throughout *Principia Ethica* in referring to "good," viz. "part," "notion," and "property," and return to his one example of the correct use of definition, viz. the "horse" example, we will see, I believe, that the shifting from one to the other of these terms produces much error and confusion. Here the shift is from the position that "good" and "yellow" are two of those "ultimate terms by reference to which whatever is capable of definition must be defined" to the position that "good" and "yellow" are "parts which are common to other wholes." In other words, Moore shifts (in mid-sentence, in fact) from the view that every "object of thought" is either a simple *notion* or capable of being analyzed into simple notions to the view that every "whole" is either a simple *part* or capable of being analyzed into its simple parts. But the main error in all this is simply the assumption that "yellow" (and consequently "good") is a "part" of something. The "arrangement" or "form" of a horse, for example, may be a "simplest notion" or "ultimate term" (in fact, "horse" may be the "simplest notion" itself), but the "arrangement" of a horse is surely not a "simplest part" of the horse, or even a part of the horse at all. Moore simply confuses the traditional theory of real definition, where *substances* are analyzed into their various qualities and properties and where different kinds of substances, e.g. natural kinds (horses, trees, etc.), mechanical complexes (engines), and sentiments (benevolence), are treated differently, to the very restricted theory of definition, where only things "composed of parts" can be analyzed.[25]

A second important thread in this passage is one that perhaps explains Moore's acceptance of the part-whole view of analysis and definition. Moore is saying here that the ultimate differences of the particulars, the ultimate terms, explains the differences in the whole, and not their specific relationship in a given whole. Thus the goodness of something would be explained by the simple something "good" and not by "good's" relationship to anything else. Thus, Moore says,

> We may admit, indeed, that when a particular thing is a part of a whole, it does possess a predicate which it would not otherwise possess—namely that it is a part of that whole. But what cannot be admitted is that this predicate alters the nature or enters into the definition of the thing which has it.[26]

Consequently, if we seek to analyze something or determine something's meaning, we must look to its parts and not to the whole or any relationships that the parts might bear to the whole. Moore rules out, on this view, any subjectivist or relational interpretation of goodness, e.g. such that "X is good" means "X is pleasing to me." In other words, goodness is a function neither of one's sentiments nor one's consciousness nor their relationship to anything else, but is a constant and independent property. He says,

> The part of a valuable whole retains exactly the same value when it is, as when it is not, a part of that whole.[27]

In short, ". . . good is good, and that is the end of the matter."[28] It is ". . . simply something which you think of or perceive, and to any one who cannot think of or perceive it, you can never, by any definition, make its nature known."[29] This view, that "good" is an absolutely constant value, is fundamental to Moore's theory, as is evidenced by the fact that it is a concise statement of the two main themes of *Principia Ethica,* viz. that all relational and egoist theories of ethics are incorrect and that ethics is absolutely independent of all other domains of inquiry and experience.

However, what is most relevant to our present discussion is that in respect to the constancy of value, it is more plausible for Moore to speak of "good" as a "part" of wholes. It makes little sense to speak of a quality of something existing absolutely independently, constantly, and objectively.[30] Consequently, Moore means by "good," when he speaks of it as a "part" of something, that it has the same relationship to that something that a "heart" of a horse has to the whole horse. We can, so to speak, (and as Moore wants us to speak) consider *"by itself"* or *"in isolation"* the "heart" of a horse.[31] But, the qualities of a horse, such as "beauty," "swiftness," and "strength," could not be judged or viewed in such a manner. All of them depend on the *arrangement* of the horse and quite obviously have no independent existence. None of them is objective and in principle, non-relational like a "heart" of a horse. Does it make sense to speak of the "beauty" or the "swiftness" of a horse remaining constant even after we remove some of his parts, e.g. his legs, heart, or head?

The question arises, then, why Moore speaks of goodness both as a "quality" and a "part." This is explained, I believe, by recognizing that Moore faces two distinct problems. One is the problem of the constancy of value—the objectivity and independence of goodness. If goodness were not objective and independent, then "reflective judgment" or "intuition" could not satisfy the position of final arbiter on questions of value and the "open question" and "absolute isolation" tests could carry no more than subjective validity. The other is the problem of the plausibility of his claim that goodness is a simple something. The constancy of value is the ultimate implication, Moore believes, of the conclusion that goodness is a simple something and the position that definition is the enumeration of the simplest parts which compose complex wholes. Since Moore *assumes* the correctness of his theory of definition, his main concern is to show that goodness is a simple something. It is to this end that Moore speaks of goodness—not as a "part" of a whole—but as a "quality" in his "yellow" analogy and as a "unique notion" in the "open question argument." Accordingly, I wish to turn to these two steps in Moore's argument in Chapter I, before considering in greater detail his theory of definition.

The Analogy of "Good" With "Yellow"

Moore recognizes the prima facie unacceptability of his general claims. It would be quite remarkable, considering the complexity of moral experience, if goodness were a simple notion, or, considering the variety and subtlety of previous ethical theories, if all or most were guilty of a common fallacy. Accordingly, Moore tries to convince us that "there is no intrinsic difficulty in the contention that 'good' denotes a simple and indefinable quality."[32] With this intention, he introduces the famous analogy of "good" with the quality "yellow." If "yellow" is a quality, is simple and indefinable, and presents no problems in respect to perception and recognition, then shouldn't it be plausible to say the same thing about "good?" So he concludes,

> There is, therefore, no intrinsic difficulty in the contention that 'good' denotes a simple and indefinable quality. There are many other instances of such qualities.[33]

And *why* are there "many other instances of such qualities"? Why, in other words, is it plausible to think that "yellow" and "good" are simple and indefinable? Because ". . . they are the ultimate terms by reference to which whatever *is* capable of definition must be defined."[34] Consequently, if every domain of enquiry presupposes "simples" in reference to which it draws its meaning, then "good" might well function as such in the ethical domain. Whether it does function as such is the primary question of *Principia Ethica:* "What is the nature of that peculiar predicate, the relation of which to other things constitutes the object of all other ethical investigations?"[35] Moore's answer is, of course, that "good" is simple, indefinable, and unanalyzable.

The analogy with yellow is offered as evidence for this conclusion. Moore analyzes the color yellow in order to show, that since "yellow" is simple and indefinable and *is recognized or shown to be such by a certain sort of mental consideration* (a mere "moment's reflection"), perhaps "good" can be shown to be simple and indefinable in the same manner. I quote the passage in full.

> Consider yellow, for example. We may try to define it, by describing its physical equivalent; we may state what kind of light-vibrations must stimulate the normal eye, in order that we may perceive it. But a moment's reflection is sufficient to shew that those light-vibrations are not themselves what we mean by yellow. *They* are not what we perceive. Indeed we should never have been able to discover their existence, unless we had first been struck by the patent difference of quality between the different colours. The most we can be entitled to say of those vibrations is that they are what corresponds in space to the yellow which we actually perceive.[36]

Moore wants us to believe that as we do not perceive light-vibrations and as we do perceive "yellow," we therefore cannot define (describe the nature of) "yellow" in terms of light-vibrations—as a "moment's reflection" by anyone who has ever perceived the color yellow will show. The obvious implication is that a moment's reflection ought to be sufficient to show to anyone who has ever perceived "good" that "good" is not something else and is therefore not definable.

Now, it is true that we do not simply perceive light-vibrations as we do the color yellow, viz. as a quality in Moore's terms or a secondary quality or substance in Hume's terms. Describing the physical equivalent of "yellow" is obviously not describing or defining the nature of the color yellow *qua* quality. Has anyone, by defining "yellow" or any other quality by its physical-science equivalent, ever thought or implied by such a definition that the physical-science equivalent was all that was meant by the quality or that the two were identical in every respect?[37]

Even in this trivially true sense, however, Moore's claim is weak. It does not even show that "yellow" is indefinable *qua* quality, but only that physical-science equivalents fail. Moore does not show, for example, that an ostensive definition would also fail to define "yellow." And this brings us to a direct sense in which Moore is in error. If Moore is correct in saying that we are entitled to say of those vibrations "that they are what corresponds in space to the yellow which we actually perceive," then we have succeeded in defining "yellow"—in what we have successfully set off "yellow," whether it is generally perceived as a quality of not, from all other things. This is certainly the object of definition according to Moore. He says,

> ... we cannot define except by an analysis, which, when carried as far as it will go, refers us to something, which is simply different from anything else, and which by that ultimate difference explains the peculiarity of the whole which we are defining.[38]

The only reason, according to Moore, that we have failed to define "yellow" is that we have failed to carry out an analysis of "yellow," i.e. to state its parts. That we can never state its parts rests on the claim that we will always recognize that "yellow" and the proposed parts are different. Of course, any weight that Moore's reasoning might have appeared to have is lost once we see that the "most important sense of defintion" precludes the possibility of defining "yellow" in the first place. The analogy to "good" is obvious. But the flaw in the analogy is that we are not constrained to conclude that "good" also is a quality or that Moore's sense of definition is the most important sense or that it is even a valid sense of definition.

The first objective of the "yellow" passage, then, is to get us to believe that there is no implausibility in the claim that "good" is a simple and indefinable quality, since there are by necessity many such qualities, e.g. "yellow." Once the plausibility is allowed, there remains (besides the *proof* that "good" is in fact simple and indefinable) only to show how it is plausible that many philosophers have previously attempted to define "good," that is, why "good" was falsely identified with something else.

Accordingly, the second objective of the passage is to get us to see that the perception of "yellow" is invariably accompanied by light-vibrations; thus, the mistake is in supposing that the light-vibrations can serve as a definition of "yellow," i.e. as a description of the real nature of "yellow."

Hume, interestingly enough, *defines* each of the natural sentiments in precisely this "fallacious" manner. He says in Book II of the *Treatise,*

> The passions of PRIDE and HUMILITY being simple and uniform impressions, 'tis impossible we can ever, by a multitude of words, give a just definition of them, or indeed of any of the passions. The utmost we can pretend to is a description of them, by an enumeration of such circumstances, as attend them.[39]

According to Hume, then, the proper method of defining "simple" notions is to describe their constant conjunctions.

In this respect, the naturalistic fallacy is the plausible mistake of identifying the *real* nature of something with what is only a constant conjunction of it. That x and y are constantly conjoined does not mean that x and y are identical or that one can serve as the description of the real nature of the other. That goodness and pleasure are constantly conjoined does not mean that goodness *is* pleasure or that pleasure is the essence (or even a *part*) of goodness. Moore says,

> It seems to me that this error has commonly been committed with regard to pleasure. Pleasure does seem to be a necessary constituent of most valuable wholes; and, since the other constituents, into which we may analyze them, may easily seem not to have value, it is natural to suppose that all the value belongs to pleasure. That this natural supposition does not follow from the premises is certain; and that it is, on the contrary, ridiculously far from the truth appears evident to 'reflective judgment.'[40]

So the error is in identifying or confusing the goodness of something with what is only a constant conjunction of it or with what seems to be a "necessary constituent" of it. Here, of course, is the precise mistake that Moore accuses Mill of making. Even if pleasure were a "necessary constituent" of all valuable things, according to Moore, it would constitute a fallacy, "ridiculously far from the truth," to identify pleasure with goodness. He says,

> Why, if good is good and indefinable, should I be held to deny that pleasure is good? Is there any difficulty in holding both to be true at once? On the contrary, there is no meaning in saying that pleasure is good, unless good is something different from pleasure.[41]

Moreover, it constitutes a *logical* fallacy:

> The point I have been labouring hitherto, the point that 'good is indefinable,' and that to deny this involves a fallacy, is a point capable of strict proof: for to deny it involves contradictions.[42]

Yet, even though the naturalistic fallacy is a fallacy capable of strict proof, Moore feels obliged to qualify his confidence in the following way:

> I should therefore be a fool if I hoped to settle one great point of controversy, now and once for all. It is extremely improbable I shall convince. It would be highly presumptuous even to hope that in the end, say two or three centuries hence, it will be agreed that pleasure is not the sole good.[43]

But, would one be a fool? Would one be presumptuous to expect to convince, if one were in fact offering the world a strict proof of the point? It strikes me that one would not. But, of course, Moore is not offering us a strict proof at all. What, then, is he doing, and why the shift from confidence to caution?

The Open Question Argument

The Open Question Argument is generally regarded as the strongest and most independent step in Moore's argument. Moore is presumably referring to this argument when he claims that the naturalistic fallacy is a fallacy capable of strict proof. But presumably, as well, it is something about this argument which leads Moore to doubt that he will convince. Let us look closely, then, at this argument, not only as to whether it proves the indefinability of "good," but also as to whether it rests upon more basic arguments or assumptions, whose weaknesses may indeed explain Moore's caution.

The Open Question Argument has two prongs: the first is supposed to show that "good" cannot have a complex meaning, and the second is supposed to show that it does have a meaning. In short, "good" is meaningful, but simple and indefinable. Moore expresses the argument in the following brief manner:

> The hypothesis that disagreement about the meaning of good is disagreement with regard to the correct analysis of a given whole, may be most plainly seen to be incorrect by consideration of the fact, whatever definition be offered, it may be always asked, with significance, of the complex so defined, whether it is itself good.[44]

In other words, when we try to define "good," we always find that the definition proposed is different in meaning from "good"–which it would not be if the definition were correct. This can be shown by the simple test of reversing the two in the form of a question. The difference is then apparent.

Now, the important question here is the question whether or not one can in fact *always* ask "with significance, of the complex so defined, whether it is itself good." If we can *always* question significantly, then the Open Question Argument is indeed a logical or formal proof of the indefinability of goodness. Otherwise, the Open Question Argument constitutes no more than a rather indecisive test of the correctness of definitions.[45] However, even if we can always question significantly, the alternative remains that the "significance" rests on grounds outside of the Open Question Argument itself. In which case, the Open Question Argument would be a valid argument, but inconclusive. It would not, in other words, constitute an independent proof of the indefinability of goodness. In this respect, the relationship of the Open Question Argument to the argument of Chapter I is such that whatever the justification (or lack of it) for the "openness" of the Open Question Argument, the same justification is essentially relevant to the claims that ethics is autonomous and that any identification of it with anything else constitutes a specific fallacy. What justification, then, does Moore offer for the "openness" of the Open Question Argument?

Goodness Is Indefinable because Simple

There are basically two distinct interpretations, as I see it, of both Moore's intent and reasoning in the Open Question Argument. One interpretation is that Moore intends by this argument to exhibit the "simplicity" of goodness–and consequently, its indefinability. The other interpretation, however, is that Moore intends by this argument to show that goodness is *always indefinable*–and consequently, simple. Perhaps, of course, there are good grounds for both interpretations. This is B. H. Baumrin's conclusion:

> What Moore did was to argue that good was indefinable, and some-

times he claims that it is indefinable *because* simple, and sometimes he argues that it is indefinable and *therefore* simple.[46]

These distinct lines of thought suggest distinct problems and their implications for Moore's basic position ought to be pursued.

In order to see that "good" is absolutely indefinable, one must (as Moore appears sometimes to be saying) simply recognize that goodness is absolutely simple. And therefore, one will see, on a "moment's reflection," that it is indefinable. On this interpretation, the Open Question Argument is, in fact, no argument at all, but only the *conditions under which* we are supposed *always* to recognize the simplicity, and therefore the indefinability, of goodness. A number of key phrases in the crucial passage in Section 13 seem to support this view:

> But whoever will attentively consider with himself what is actually before his mind when he asks the question 'Is pleasure (or whatever it may be) after all good?' can easily satisfy himself that he is not merely wondering whether pleasure is pleasant. And if he will try this experiment with each suggested definition in succession, he may become expert enough to recognize that in every case he has before his mind a unique object, with regard to the connection of which with any other object, a distinct question may be asked. Every one does in fact understand the question 'Is this good?' When he thinks of it, his state of mind is different from what it would be, where he asked 'Is this pleasant, or desired, or approved?' It has a distinct meaning for him, even though he may not recognize in what respect it is distinct. Whenever he thinks of 'intrinsic value,' or 'intrinsic worth,' or says that a thing 'ought to exist,' he has before his mind the unique object—the unique property of things—which I mean by 'good.' Everybody is constantly aware of this notion, although he may never become aware at all that it is different from other notions of which he is also aware. But, for correct ethical reasoning, it is extremely important that he should become aware of this fact; and, as soon as the nature of the problem is clearly understood, there should be little difficulty in advancing so far in analysis.[47]

The key phrases are: "... attentively consider with himself what is actually before his mind when he asks the question," "... in every case he has before his mind a unique object," "(Good) has a distinct meaning for him," and "Everybody is constantly aware of this notion."

Now, on what grounds is Moore justified in claiming that "... in every case he has before his mind a unique object"? Surely, not because some attempted definitions have in fact failed. Even if all previous (and future) definitions were to fail the test of reversibility, it would not prove that "in every case" we had before our minds a unique object. Moore is obviously drawing support for the "always" or "in every case", i.e., for the formal validity of his position, from outside the Open Question Argument itself. And the following chapters of *Principia Ethica,* especially Chapter VI, make it clear just what this support is, viz. "intuition" or "reflective judgment."[48] The assumption here is that if we attentively consider what is actually *before our minds* when we ask ourselves whether something is the definition of "good," then we will recognize in every case that we have a unique object before our mind. But there is no logical argument here. Where are the contradictions that Moore claims will result from the denial of the simplicity and indefinability of goodness? He is not arguing here that a logical fallacy is involved in the acceptance of a suggested definition of goodness, but only that in every case we will recognize that goodness is unique and therefore different from the suggested definition. And how is it that we can be certain that in *every* case our attempt at definition will fail? Not, and this is the point, because defining goodness is a logical impossibility, but rather because goodness is recognized to be the sort of thing which is unsusceptible to definition, viz. a unique object.

The only formal or strict validity of which the Open Question Argument can boast is that which we credit to our "intuition" or "reflective judgment." But if we do not accept the existence of such a mode of cognition, or at least, do not accept its pretence to reliability, then the Open Question Argument is reduced to the merest form of subjective appeal. It is an appeal to those persons who view goodness—perhaps because they are simply unaware of the complexities of moral experience—as simple, as a unique object of thought. Indeed, this is the singular conclusion of that important passage:

> Everybody is constantly aware of this notion, although he may never become aware at all that it is different from other notions of which he is also aware. But, for correct ethical reasoning, it is extremely important that he should become aware of this fact. . .[49]

But it is precisely this "fact," as crucial to Moore's argument as it is, that he simply assumes, and never proves. He says,

> And if he will try this experiment with each suggested definition in succession, he may become expert enough to recognize that in every case he has before his mind a unique object, with regard to the connection of which with any other object, a distinct question may be asked.[50]

To be sure, in order to evaluate a proposed definition of goodness, one must have, prior to the proposal, some knowledge or recognition of goodness—otherwise, questioning the proposed definition would be no more *significant* than any other question stemming from ignorance. I would imagine, as well, that the "object" to be defined would have to be "unique" in Moore's sense here, viz. "a unique object, with regard to the connection of which with any other object, a distinct question may be asked." An admittedly complex object or notion, "university", for example, is unique in Moore's sense. The point is simply that being *unique* has nothing to do with being *simple* or *indefinable*.

What Moore assumes, then, is not merely that goodness is "unique," but that it is unique in a very special way. Moore assumes that the *real* nature of goodness is such that it is incapable of definition, and not merely that it functions "before our minds" as a "unique notion." The former, stronger assumption is not in the least bit evidenced by the Open Question Argument. On the contrary, it provides the sole support for that "argument." In other words, only if we could, by means of our "intuition" or "reflective judgment," recognize that the *real nature* of goodness was absolutely *simple,* would we be justified in claiming that goodness was indefinable "always" or "in every case." But "intuition," or "reflective judgment," is powerless to exhibit the *real nature*—if we mean by that what Moore does, viz. the simplest parts which invariably compose a given whole—of anything at all. At best, through "intuition" one might recognize that he has before his mind a "unique object," a "unique notion," but not by that a "simplest thing." "Horse" and "university" may well appear as "unique objects" or "notions" before our minds, yet this provides us with no evidence for claiming that they are in fact "unique things" or "simple wholes"—or that we cannot define them.

In sum, if the Open Question Argument is interpreted as proving that goodness is indefinable *because* simple, then it quite clearly fails. For the sense in which goodness might be recognized as "unique" *before our minds* has nothing to do with its having no parts or being incapable of analysis or, in short, of being indefinable. "Atom," for example, may appear as a unique object before our minds, yet the question whether it *is* such is quite distinct from the questions whether it is ultimately composed of neutrons, neutrinos, etc., and whether, even if it is an absolutely simple whole (whatever sense that may make), it is yet susceptible to definition in some significant sense.

More generally, the questions whether something is a "simple notion," whether something is a "simple thing" (in the sense of not being composed of any "parts"), and whether something can be defined, are three distinct questions. Moore mistakenly believes either that they are strictly synonymous or that the entailments holding between the three are such that the proof of one constitutes the proof of the others. And his confusing these questions is the main reason, I believe, why Moore is so confident about the correctness of his position. There would be little cause for dispute, if one were to claim, for example, that "atom" functions as a "unique notion" or "object" before our minds—yet, it is simply incorrect to claim that "atom" is an absolutely simple thing, a simplest whole. If "simple notion" meant exactly the same thing as "simple thing," then every intellectual domain would be guilty of innumerable basic fallacies.

Indeed, it appears to me that one of the fundamental tasks of, and perhaps the greatest impetus to, intellectual and scientific thought, is to *analyze* those "unique objects of thought," e.g. "neutrino," "vacuum," "space," "pain," "pleasure," "love," "hatred," "yellow," and so on, which in fact result, either by discovery or creation, from all intellectual and scientific activity and provide as such the source of meaning in their respective domains. Consequently, the interesting question is whether we can *analyze, understand, identify,* goodness, and not whether we can distinguish it before our minds from all other notions. The question, in short, concerns the thinking which underlies Moore's belief that the real nature of goodness cannot be analyzed, identified, understood—*by means of definition.*

22

Goodness Is Simple Because Indefinable

Consequently, our second line of interpretation of the Open Question Argument, .viz. that goodness is simple *because* indefinable, appears to express more justly Moore's intent by that argument. Specifically, we are questioning, then, whether the Open Question Argument proves, or exhibits, the indefinability of goodness, that goodness is "always" or "in every case" indefinable.

In order to define goodness (or anything else) in the "most important sense of 'definition',"[51] one must state the *parts* which compose it. And in order to define the *real* nature of goodness, one must state its *simplest parts.*[52] Now, in order to determine whether a proposed definition of goodness is correct, one must determine whether the proposed definition is "absolutely and entirely the same with goodness."[53] One must, in short, determine whether the proposition " 'goodness' is 'the proposed complex of simplest parts' " is analytical, which for Moore means the proposed complex provides "exactly the same information about"[54] goodness as 'goodness' provides for it.

Moore's Theory of Definition and The Open Question Argument

Now, I certainly agree with Moore that goodness is "always" and "in every case" indefinable—*in his sense of definition.* But this conclusion does not in the least favor his general position. On the contrary, it points to the weaknesses and confusions of his theory of definition. The only reason which one can formulate for the indefinability of goodness in terms of the Open Question Argument is directly dependent upon the correctness of the view that definition is the enumeration of the simplest parts of complex wholes. But even assuming that it is theoretically possible to enumerate the "simplest parts" (or even one simplest part) of things, one could *never* be certain that his enumeration was exhaustive, ruling out, as Moore does, stipulative and observably identical definitions. In terms of the Open Question Argument, it appears that not only goodness, but no term whatsoever is definable. For according to the Open Question Argument, our enumeration of "simplest parts" must be exhaustive; it must, as Moore says, be "absolutely and entirely the same with goodness."[55] It must, in short, be such that ". . . anyone can easily convince himself by inspection that the predicate of this proposition—'good'—is positively [identical] with the notion. . . which enters into its subject."[56] But how, on these conditions, is such a mental identity possible?

Moore's Chimaera Example

Moore provides us with one example, besides the "horse" example discussed below, of definition or analysis by enumeration of "parts." Moore says,

> We can, for instance, make a man understand what a chimaera is, although he has never heard of one or seen one. You can tell him that it is an animal with a lioness's head and body, with a goat's head growing from the middle of its back, and with a snake in place of a tail. But here the object which you are describing is a complex object; it is entirely composed of parts, with which we are all perfectly familiar—a snake, a goat, a lioness; and we know, too, the manner in which those parts are to be put together, be-

23

cause we know what is meant by the middle of a lioness's back, and where her tail is wont to grow.[57]

Keeping in mind that Moore has ruled out verbal or dictionary definitions and consequently is here concerned only with "real" definitions, a number of objections to this example can be raised. In order to define (describe) the *real* nature of something, one must enumerate the *simplest parts* which invariably compose it. Now, "snake," "goat," and "lioness," are certainly not the simplest parts of a chimaera. Moore is correct in saying that we can tell someone that a chimaera is ". . . an animal with a lioness's head and body, and with a goat's head, etc., etc.", but we are not by that describing the *real* nature of a chimaera to him in Moore's sense, i.e. telling him what is "absolutely and entirely the same with (chimaera)."[58] Consequently, Moore's chimaera example is a failure in a double sense: on the one hand, since it does in fact fail, there is no reason for us to admit that a *real* definition in Moore's sense is possible at all, and on the other hand, since we are not in the least constrained to admit that goodness is the same sort of thing as a chimaera, (even if this example did provide us with an instance of *real* definition in terms of simplest parts) we are not constrained to admit its relevance to ethical theory.

Moreover, Moore avoids, by this example, two of the more interesting questions involved in definition, real or otherwise, viz. How can we be certain that our definition (description) conveys the idea of the whole being defined to someone who has no idea of some of the "parts" or "terms" of our definition? If one has never seen a chimaera, it is highly questionable whether we can assume, as Moore does, giving him the above list of parts, viz. "a lioness's head, etc." that he would know,

too, the manner in which those parts are to be put together, because we know what is meant by the middle of a lioness's back, and where her tail is wont to grow.[59]

The chimaera example presupposes, in other words, that we are all familiar with a chimaera, and being familiar, recognize that such and such are in fact the "parts" of it. But if we assume prior familiarity, the point of the example is utterly lost, namely, to "make a man understand what a chimaera is, although he has never heard of one or seen one."[60]

And the same reasoning is sufficient to show the irrelevance of the chimaera example to the second question above. Briefly, if one has never seen a goat, and consequently his tail, I do not know how we could go about defining or describing it to him by an enumeration of parts, simple or otherwise. We could not, in short, even describe "where (his) tail is wont to grow."[61]

But perhaps the most interesting point about the chimaera example is not its possible irrelevance to the question of definition in ethics, or even its possible irrelevance to the question of definition itself, but the fact that a chimaera is a *non-natural* something. According to Moore, we are supposed to be concerned only with definition "in the most important sense of that word." It is noteworthy, then, considering the fact that Moore provides us with only two instances of "real" definition, that one of them is highly artificial (non-natural?) and obscure. It is true that the subject of Moore's other example of real definition, his "horse" example, is unobscure and admittedly "natural." Yet, if we consider this latter example in some detail, we will see, I believe, that it is only if we view "horse" in the same way as we do a chimaera, viz. from an artificial, non-natural point of view, can we make even partial sense of Moore's theory of definition.

Moore's Theory of Definition and "Natural" Objects or Ideas

Before considering the details of the "horse" example, however, it is worth re-emphasizing the central importance of Moore's theory of definition and significance that any criticisms of it will necessarily carry.

It must be remembered that the main intention of Chapter I is to prove two distinct but related points. Moore wants to prove, on the one hand, that ethics is strictly autonomous and, on the other, that there is a logical fallacy common to most ethical theories. The strict proof of both claims follows, believes Moore, from the strict proof of the indefinability and simplicity of "good." He says,

> ... the point that 'good is indefinable,' and that to deny this involves a fallacy, is a point capable of strict proof: for to deny it involves contradictions.[62]

If "good" is strictly simple and indefinable, and "good" is the "notion upon which all Ethics depends,"[63] then ethics has no formal or primary relationship to anything else and any attempt to relate it, constitutes a fallacy. The point here is that "good" must be absolutely (formally, strictly, logically) indefinable and simple, if Moore's claims are to have sweeping validity. And it is this sense of "good" which Moore believes is supported by his theory of definition.

We considered above[64] one example, the simple quality "yellow," to which Moore's theory of definition is supposed *not* to apply. Its not applying shows, according to Moore, that "yellow" is indefinable. He says,

> My point is that 'good' is a simple notion, just as 'yellow' is a simple notion; that, just as you cannot, by any manner of means, explain to any one who does not already know it, what yellow is, so you cannot explain what good is. Definitions of the kind that I was asking for, definitions which describe the real nature of the object or notion denoted by a word, and which do not merely tell us what the word is used to mean, are only possible when the object or notion in question is something complex.[65]

Understanding the nature and purpose of definition is, then, a preliminary condition to determining the question whether "good," or anything else, is definable. And since "Definitions of the kind that (Moore) was asking for, definitions which describe the real nature of the object or notion denoted by a word"[66] is exhibited by the "horse" example, we should find in that example, which Mary Warnock rightly characterized as "obscure," but wrongly as unimportant,[67] the substance of the two main themes of *Principia Ethica*. For Moore's analysis of "horse" is essentially reducible to his analysis of "good" and consequently to the main themes of *Principia Ethica*. He says,

> A horse's simplest terms are simply something which you think of

or perceive, and to any one who cannot think of or perceive them, you can never, by any definition, make their nature known.[68]

With appropriate substitutions it becomes clear that accepting Moore's theory of definition is, tantamount to accepting his "naturalistic fallacy" claim. The above could just as well read as follows:

"Good" is simply something which you think of or perceive, and to any one who cannot think or perceive it, you can never, by any definition, make its nature known.

And since, "simply perceiving" something turns out to be "intuiting" something,[69] according to Moore, we have here the support for the positive, as well as the negative, thesis of *Principia Ethica*. If "good" can *only* be known by intuition, then all judgments of the form "X is good in itself" must therefore "remain unaffected by any conclusions we may reach about the nature of reality."[70] And if "good" cannot be defined, then any attempt constitutes a basic fallacy. There you have it. Any doubt about the central importance of Moore's theory of definition should now be removed. And if I succeed below in exhibiting the weakness and confusion in this aspect of his work, then I feel that I have succeeded in casting doubt on the substance of Moore's general claims.

Moore's "Horse" Example

We should now be in a position to consider the details of Moore's "horse" example. He says,

We may mean when we define 'horse' that a certain object, which we all of us know, is composed in a certain manner: that it has four legs, a head, a heart, a liver, etc., etc., all of them arranged in definite relations to one another. It is in this sense that I deny good to be definable. I say that it is not composed of any parts, which we can substitute for it in our minds when we are thinking of it.[71]

The point of this example, i.e. in trying to show us that "horse" is indefinable, is obviously to show that "good" is not likewise definable. "Good" is indefinable, because it does not have, like "horse," "any parts, which we can substitute in our minds when we are thinking of it." "Horse," then, like a "chimaera," *does* have parts which we can substitute in our minds when we are thinking of it. But does it? This thought experiment does not work for me. Moore gives us the modest list of "four legs, a head, a heart, a liver, etc., etc.." But the "etc., etc." is very important here. To carry out the thought experiment which would confirm his view of definition, we must know all the parts. We cannot allow an "etc., etc.," for if it were to turn out that in the case of every *natural* object one must simply make do with an incomplete enumeration, then goodness might be indefinable on Moore's own terms *because* it is a natural object—and not because it is an absolute simple.

Moreover, according to Moore, a *real* definition is successful only when we have enumerated all the *simplest* parts of an object. He says,

And so it is with all objects, not previously known, which we are able to define: they are all complex; all composed of parts, which

26

may themselves, in the first instance, be capable of similar definition, but which must in the end be reducible to simplest parts, which can no longer be defined.[72]

Now, where are we to find these "simplest parts"? Certainly, none of those "parts" listed by Moore qualifies. A head of a horse has eyes, hair, ears, etc., etc. The eyes of a head of a horse have color, a cornea, a pupil, an iris, etc., etc. Quite obviously, such an analysis could go on indefinitely.[73] Moore believes, however, that the further we carry such an analysis, the closer we get to the *real* nature of "horse." But, if this were the case, the real nature of any object would be either a hopeless obscurity or a mass of Democritean atoms or Leibnizian monads or some such *metaphysical* likeness. And everything might well be, *au fond,* nothing but serene monads or swarming atoms—but this is all beside the point. This is not what we are talking about when we speak of the *definition* or the *real nature* of "horse" or "goodness." "Man," for example, has been defined as "rational biped." Certainly, "rationality" and "two-leggedness" are neither the "simplest parts" of "man" nor exhaustively descriptive. "Rational biped" is rather an attempt to provide (however unsatisfactorily) a sufficient set of properties which distinguish the class "man" from all other classes. Consequently, rather than make the impossible claim that,

> You can give a definition of a horse, because a horse has many different properties and qualities, all of which you can enumerate.[74]

Moore might correctly argue that,

> You can give a definition of "horse" because the word "horse" denotes something which has many different properties, a sufficient set of which when stated will set the class of horses apart from all other classes.[75]

Indeed, had Moore embraced this latter position, he not only would have had at his disposal a method of definition with practical application (so as to test the validity of his claims), but would have seen that many "naturalists" were not at all guilty of the "naturalistic fallacy"—because they simply were not concerned to define goodness by an exhaustive enumeration. Mill, for example, is surely not concerned, in attempting to define goodness, to propose that pleasure is "absolutely and entirely the same with goodness."[76] He is rather claiming that pleasure alone is sufficient to set off goodness from all other things. Mill may well be mistaken in claiming this, but he is not therefore guilty of a *special* fallacy. He would be guilty of the special fallacy, dubbed by Moore the "naturalistic fallacy," only if the object of definition were in fact exhaustive enumeration resulting in an identity—for it is only in these terms and on these conditions that goodness is "shown" to be simple by Moore in the first place.

The Basic Error in Moore's Theory of Definition

Moore appears to believe that since (if) every complex whole is ultimately composed of absolutely simple terms or parts, then (a) "the most important sense of definition" is the enumeration of those terms or parts and (b) the simple terms and parts are consequently not susceptible to "real" analysis or definition. This helps us understand the philosophical origins of his theory of definition, but it does not answer the curious question why Moore, in the face of so many practical and theoretical difficulties, is convinced that his sense of definition is a workable one. Perhaps the answer to this question lies in the remarkably confused last sentence of the "horse" passage. Moore says,

> We might think just as clearly and correctly about a horse, if we thought of all its parts and their arrangement instead of thinking of the whole: we could, I say, think how a horse differed from a donkey just as well, just as truly, in this way, as now we do, only not so easily; but there is nothing whatsoever which we could so substitute for good; and that is what I mean, when I say that good is indefinable.[77]

Moore is here adding a key proviso or qualification. It is that when we think of a horse's parts, i.e. of his properties and qualities, as opposed to thinking of the *whole* horse, we must think of them in a certain "arrangement." This qualification adds some plausibility to his position, but does it improve matters? I believe not. If our object is to enumerate those parts which, when arranged in a certain manner, are substitutable in our minds for the complex notion of a horse, definition appears theoretically possible to carry out, at least, but at the same time, Moore's error is pointed up. If we had a list of the parts of a horse and attempted to substitute them in our mind in a certain manner or in a definite order or arrangement, we would have, to be sure, a horse. But that is because a horse is a heart, liver, and an indefinite number of other properties and qualities *arranged* or *ordered* in a certain manner. What Moore promised to show, and what he must show in order to support his subsequent claims, is that "horse" can be defined, its nature can be exhibited, by the enumeration of those parts which invariably compose it—not by the enumeration of those parts in a certain order or arrangement—for that is exactly in what respect and in what manner we begin our thought experiment and attempt a definition. Indeed, is there any conceivable difference between "all of a horse's parts and their arrangement" and a "whole horse"?

Moore does believe that there is a difference. And assuming (a) and (b) above, Moore's belief is justified. But even if (a) and (b) were correct, it would not follow that the Open Question Argument was valid. In other words, even if the view that the "real" nature of something were directly dependent upon the distinct natures of the individual parts which compose it, it would not follow that a "conceptual" test is in any way relevant to this distinction. But, in order that there be a definition in Moore's sense, we must have on the one side, a complex whole and on the other side, a complex of parts, and the two sides must be in some sense conceptually distinct. Otherwise, what would be the purpose of the thought experiment (Open Question Argument) designed *to test* our proposed definitions or, indeed, of definition itself, on Moore's theory?

Conclusion

What Moore appears to have assumed, then, is that *in principle* we can give a definition of a natural kind, e.g. horse, in terms of its most fundamental perceptual and cognitive parts, e.g. head, eyes, heart, shape, color, and so on—just as a chimaera, an admittedly non-natural object, is described. And this assumption seems to be based on the more basic assumption that all things are either simple or "reducible to simplest parts, which can no longer be defined."[78] If Moore were correct in these assumptions, he could validly infer that the object of definition in ethics is a similar reduction. And if it turned out that some notion(s) in ethics was incapable of such reduction, then one could validly conclude that the notion or thing in question was simple and indefinable. These are, I believe, Moore's assumptions and the inferences and conclusions which he draws from them. Once they are recognized for what they are and the various threads which bind them exhibited, the "critical threat" of Chapter I of *Principia Ethica* virtually dissolves.

To this end, I have tried to show that, even in principle, one *cannot* give a definition of a natural kind in terms of its most fundamental perceptual and cognitive terms. Consequently, that Moore's theory of definition is not the "most important sense of definition" in ethics and that, by employing a sense of definition which is inappropriate to the content of naturalistic ethical theories, Moore prejudges the case against them. The immediate consequences of my criticisms are a) that Moore's "naturalistic fallacy" is simply inapplicable to "naturalistic ethical theories," since it rests upon the mistaken inference that the object of definition in ethics is a reduction of primary ethical terms, e.g. goodness, to their simplest parts or terms and b) that Moore's argument in Chapter I of *Principia Ethica* provides no support for the positive contention that ethcis is strictly autonomous, since, solely on the basis of the argument there, goodness may indeed be a *natural* something.

The question remains, then, whether goodness is in fact a "non-natural" property, as Moore argues in Chapter II of *Principia Ethica*. If goodness is a non-natural property, then the "naturalistic fallacy" can be interpreted as the general fallacy of identifying or confusing goodness with what is by nature different from it. And the specific fallacy of "naturalistic ethical theories" would now be the fallacy of identifying (irrespective of any specific use of definition) goodness with any natural property or quality. Accordingly, I would now like to turn to Chapter II of *Principia Ethica* and to Moore's second main line of reasoning in support of the negative thesis that there is a basic fallacy common to most previous ethical theories and the positive one that ethics is strictly autonomous.

[1]*Principia*, p. 14.

[2]*Ibid.*, p. viii.

[3]*International Journal of Ethics*, Oct. 1903, p. 116.

[4]*Principia*, p. 39.

[5]*Ibid.*, p. 114.

[6]*Ibid.*, p. 38.

[7]*Ibid.*, p. 40.

[8]*Ibid.*, p. 144.

[9]*Ibid.*, p. 15.

[10]*Ibid.*, p. 37.

[11]*Ibid.*, p. 6.

[12]Mary Warnock, *Ethics Since 1900*, London, Oxford University Press, 1960, pp. 20-21.

[13]Moore does consider the possible ambiguity and some of the problematic implications of the view that goodness is a "quality," in his essay, "Is Goodness a Quality," in *Philosophical Papers*, London, George Allen & Unwin, LTD, 1963. He says, referring to his intent in *Principia Ethica*, "I meant merely that the character of being worth having for its own sake *was* a character and was *not* a relational property." (p. 97) And since "worth having for its own sake" is synonymous with "intrinsically good," Moore is here saying that goodness as a *quality* refers to the *intrinsic nature* of good things. Consequently, this essay does not bear directly on our present concern. The general question whether goodness refers to "intrinsic nature," is secondary to the question whether there are in fact "qualities" (and consequently, "intrinsic natures") in Moore's sense of simple and complex. In other words, the question whether goodness is simple, indefinable, and unanalyzable is contingent, in Chapter I of *Principia Ethica*, upon whether "qualities," or "intrinsic natures," are susceptible to analysis (definition) in terms of their "simplest parts."

[14]*Principia*, p. 10.

[15]*Ibid.*, pp. 16-17.

[16]*Ibid.*, pp. 7-8.

[17]Mary Warnock, *Ethics Since 1900*, London, Oxford University Press, 1960, pp. 24.

[18]*Principia*, p. 9.

[19]*Ibid.*, p. 38.

[20]W. Frankena, "The Naturalistic Fallacy," in *Readings in Ethical Theory*, ed. by W. Sellars and J. Hospers, New York, Appleton-Century-Crofts, 1952.

[21]*Principia*, p. 114.

[22]*Ibid.*, p. 9.

[23]*Ibid.*, p. 10.

[24]*Ibid.*, p. 9-10.

[25]B. H. Baumrin, in his essay, "Is There A Naturalistic Fallacy?," *American*

Philosophical Quarterly, Vol. 5, Number 2, 1968, pp. 80-84 (especially p. 83), exhibits this shift in Moore's thinking and argument in a brief, but convincing manner.

[26]*Principia*, p. 33.

[27]*Ibid.*, p. 30.

[28]*Ibid.*, p. 6.

[29]*Ibid.*, p. 7.

[30]From a different direction, C. D. Broad makes this point in his essay, "Moore's Ethical Doctrines" in *The Philosophy of G. E. Moore*, ed. by Paul Arthur Schilpp, New York, Tudor Publishing Company, 1952. He says there, in reference to Moore's criterion of "naturalness," viz. "capable of existing in time" (*Principia*, p. 41.): "Now it seems to me that *every* characteristic of a natural object answers to Moore's criterion of non-naturalness, and that *no* characteristic could possibly be natural in his sense." This, I take it, is to say that in so far as "good" is like the quality "yellow," then it makes no sense to speak of it as "non-natural," i.e. as constant and independent.

[31]*Principia*, p. 93.

[32]*Ibid.*, p. 10.

[33]*Ibid.*, p. 10.

[34]*Ibid.*, p. 10.

[35]*Ibid.*, p. 37.

[36]*Ibid.*, p. 10.

[37]Susan Stebbing, in her essay, "Furniture of the Earth," in *Philosophy of Science*, ed. by Arthur Danto and Sidney Morgenbesser, New York, The World Publishing Company, 1963, seems to be criticizing Eddington for committing this sort of basic mistake. Eddington supposedly confuses his physical-science terms with ordinary terms, or the elements of physical science with the objects of ordinary experience. Stebbing's criticism is reminiscent of Moore in that she condemns an unnamed host of scientists for committing an artless linguistic fallacy, while Moore condemns an unnamed host of ethical philosophers for committing an artless logical error. Stebbing's suggested "solution" to her discovered fallacy, moreover, is likewise reminiscent of Moore. Stebbing points to the uniqueness of linguistic norms, while Moore to certain notions. Unfortunately our pursuit of this parallel must rest here. It should suffice to say (at least for all those who have read Eddington) that the issues on his side are neither simple nor simple-minded. See Sir Arthur Eddington, *The Philosophy of Physical Science*, Ann Arbor, The University of Michigan Press, 1958.

[38]*Principia*, p. 10.

[39]David Hume, *A Treatise of Human Nature*, ed. L. A. Selby-Bigge, Oxford, Clarendon Press, 1960, p. 277. Hereafter I shall refer to this work as *Treatise*.

[40]*Principia*, p. 93-94.

[41]*Ibid.*, p. 14.

[42]*Ibid.*, p. 77.

[43]*Ibid.*, p. 76.

[44]*Ibid.*, p. 15.

[45]George F. Hourani is one among many ethical theorists who accept the case by case validity of the Open Question Argument or Test, but who reject its "logical" validity. Hourani is confident that he can find a *definition* of goodness which is acceptable in terms of the Open Question Argument, even on a case by case basis, entails the acceptance of Moore's theory of definition and the relevance of his "verbal-cognitive" approach to moral enquiry. George F. Hourani, *Ethical Value*, London, George Allen & Union LTD., 1956, especially pp. 87-90.

[46]B. H. Baumrin, "Is There A Naturalistic Fallacy?," *American Philosophical Quarterly*, Vol. 5, Number 2, 1968, p. 85.

[47]*Principia*, pp. 16-17.

[48]*Ibid.*, especially pp. 187-190.

[49]*Ibid.*, p. 17.

[50]*Ibid.*, p. 16.

[51]*Ibid.*, p. 9.

[52]*Ibid.*, p. 8.

[53]*Ibid.*, p. 10.

[54]*Ibid.*, p. 16.

[55]*Ibid.*, p. 10.

[56]*Ibid.*, p. 16.

[57]*Ibid.*, p. 7.

[58]*Ibid.*, p. 10.

[59]*Ibid.*, p. 7.

[60]*Ibid.*, p. 7.

[61]*Ibid.*, p. 7.

[62]*Ibid.*, p. 77.

[63]*Ibid.*, p. 37.

[64]Cf. pp. 30-37.

[65]*Principia*, p. 7.

[66]*Ibid.*, p. 7.

[67]Mary Warnock, *Ethics Since 1900*, London, Oxford University Press, 1960, p. 20-21.

[68]*Principia*, p. 7.

[69]"By saying that a proposition is self-evident, we mean emphatically that its appearing so to us, is *not* the reason why it is true: for we mean that it has absolutely no reason," (*Principia*, p. 143.)

[70]Cf. pp. 10-11.

[71]*Principia*, p. 8.

[72]*Ibid.*, pp. 7-8.

[73]Curiously enough, Moore seems never to have attempted a definition in his sense of definition. He says later in the "horse" passage, "We *might* think just as clearly and correctly about a horse, if we thought of all its parts and their arrangement instead of thinking of the whole. . . " (italics mine) Besides the fact that the impossible problems facing his theory would have become immediately apparent had he ever attempted such a definition, saying that "We *might* think just as clearly, etc." implies that he never did attempt it himself.

[74]*Principia*, p. 7.

[75]B. H. Baumrin, "Is There A Naturalistic Fallacy?," *American Philosophical Quarterly*, Vol. 5, Number 2, 1968, p. 80.

[76]*Principia*, p. 10.

[77]*Ibid.*, p. 8.

[78]*Ibid.*, p. 8.

CHAPTER TWO

Introduction

The object of the present chapter is to evaluate Moore's argument in Chapter II of *Principia Ethica*, purporting to prove that goodness is a "non-natural" property. The independent importance of this second step in Moore's general argument is obvious. If goodness is a "non-natural" property, then ethics is formally distinguishable from other domains of enquiry and any identification of goodness with a "natural" property or properties constitutes a basic fallacy. If valid, then, the argument in Chapter II provides by itself a strong basis for both the positive and negative theses of *Principia Ethica*. What is not obvious, however, is the relationship that this argument in Chapter II bears to the important argument of Chapter I. For instance: Is the view that ethics is formally autonomous dependent upon the position that goodness is strictly indefinable and unanalyzable (Chapter I) or upon the position that goodness has a unique nature (Chapter II)? Or: Is the view that "naturalistic ethical theories" rest on a fundamental mistake dependent upon the position that goodness is a simple property (Chapter I) or upon the position that goodness is a "non-natural" property (Chapter II)—or upon both, perhaps? It is unclear, in other words, whether Chapter II constitutes an independent proof of the general claims of

Principia Ethica or whether it is a second and necessary step in Moore's general argument.

The argument of Chapter I certainly seems to provide an independent basis for the view that ethics is formally autonomous. If goodness is strictly indefinable and unanalyzable, then,

> all truths of the form "This is good in itself: are logically independent of any truth about what exists. No ethical proposition of this form is such that, if a certain thing exists, it is true, whereas, if that thing does not exist, it is false. All such ethical truths are true, *whatever the nature of the world may be.*[1]

What Moore appears to be saying here is that any theory which rests upon an analysis or definition of goodness is fallacious—not because goodness is a peculiar non-natural object, but because it is simple, unanalyzable, and indefinable. The argument in Chapter I appears to be directed, then, against what Moore believes is a commonly accepted method of argument and justification in ethical enquiry, namely, argument by definition and analysis. It is directed against any attempt to employ this method in resolving questions of primary ethical value. But contrary to what has become accepted opinion today, there is nothing in the argument of Chapter I which is directed against a specific "type" of ethical theory. For example, in respect to the argument there, a theory which holds that goodness is a natural, but simple something is quite unobjectionable. The clear implication in Chapter I is that further arguments will be provided to show that goodness is neither a "natural" nor "metaphysical" something. Taken literally, Moore's words in the important Section 12 of Chapter I make it clear that the argument there does not constitute a critique restricted to naturalistic ethics." He says,

> As for the reasons why good is not to be considered a natural object, they may be reserved for discussion in another place. But, for the present, it is sufficient to notice this: Even if it were a natural object, that would not alter the nature of the fallacy nor diminish its importance one whit. All that I have said about it would remain quite equally true: only the name which I have called it would not be so appropriate as I think it is.[2]

And indeed, Chapters II, III, and IV of *Principia Ethica* are appropriately titled "Naturalistic Ethics," "Hedonism," and "Metaphysical Ethics" respectively. Moore attempts to show in turn that each of these "types" of ethical theory is an instance of the general fallacy, which he has misleadingly labelled "the naturalistic fallacy." But it remains unclear whether they are instances of this general fallacy because each of them attempts a definition or analysis of goodness or because each of them fails to recognize the "non-natural" nature of goodness. In fact, Moore's own introduction to Chapter II exemplifies this problem in a brief statement. He says there,

> The subject of the present chapter is, then, ethical theories which declare that no intrinsic value is to be found except in the possession of some one *natural* property, other than pleasure; and which declare this because it is supposed that to be 'good' *means* to pos-

sess the property in question.[3]

Is Moore saying here that naturalistic ethical theories are fallacious because they fail to identify goodness with what it really is, viz. some one "non-natural" property, or because they attempt to identify goodness in the first place? In other words, are naturalistic ethical theories fallacious in Moore's view because of the negative claim that " 'good' itself is not a natural property"[4] (Chapter II), or because of the negative claim that good is indefinable and unanalyzable (Chapter II)?

The Confusion of the Non-natural with the Natural

The difficulty in distinguishing and dealing with these two distinct lines of thought is magnified in a crucial passage in Chapter II. Moore is there attempting to prove that " 'good' itself is not a natural property," but he begins with one line of thought and ends with another. He begins by saying,

Can we imagine 'good' as existing *by itself* in time, and not merely as a property of some natural object? For myself, I cannot so imagine it, whereas with the greater number of properties of objects—those which I call the natural properties—their existence does not seem to me to be independent of the existence of those objects. They are, in fact, rather parts of which the object is made up than mere predicates which attach to it. If they were all taken away, no object would be left, not even a bare substance: for they are in themselves substantial and give to the object all the substance that it has. But this is not so with good.[5]

The clear implication of this 'proof' of the non-natural nature of goodness is that the failure of naturalistic ethics to recognize this 'fact' is the basis of its misdirection and fallaciousness. In other words, the belief that goodness is a natural property—irrespective of any attempt to define it—appears to be the distinctive error of naturalistic ethics. "Can we imagine 'good' as existing *by itself* in time?" If not, according to Moore, goodness is "non-natural" and any failure to recognize this constitutes a basic fallacy.

Carl Wellman, in fact, believes that the "most obvious interpretation" of the naturalistic fallacy is,

the confusion of the nonnatural with the natural. Moore contends that the characteristics for which ethical words stand are fundamentally different from any natural characteristics. The error of ethical naturalism is looking within nature for the ethical facts which actually belong to quite another realm of being.[6]

But we need only continue to the conclusion of the above passage of Moore's to see that it is far from obvious what Moore believes is the "real" fallacy of naturalistic ethics. He says,

if indeed good were a feeling, as some would have us believe, then it would exist in time. But that is why to call it so is to commit the naturalistic fallacy. It will always remain pertinent to ask, whether the feeling itself is good; and if so, then good cannot itself be identical with any feeling.[7]

Here in one sentence Moore is saying that to hold that goodness "exists in time," i.e. that it is a "natural" something, is to commit the naturalistic fallacy. But in the very next sentence, he says that "It will always be pertinent to ask, whether the feeling itself is good," i.e. whether one has failed the Open Question Argument. And, of course, the difference between these two arguments is vast. The Open Question Argument supports a strict, formal sense of the "naturalistic fallacy." This is the sense of the "fallacy" which Frankena has called the "definist fallacy"[8] and which we have indeed seen to be based on Moore's theory of definition. And though this interpretation of the "fallacy" is historically and philosophically significant, we have seen also that it has no special relevance for "naturalistic ethics."

The argument in Chapter II, however, does seem to carry such special relevance for naturalistic ethics in Moore's mind. He specifically emphasizes this relevance while summarizing his results in Chapter V. He concludes there,

> So much, then, for the first step in our ethical method, the step which established that good is good and nothing else whatever, and that Naturalism was a fallacy.[9]

But there seems to be no clear reason to assume that Moore's argument to the effect that goodness is "non-natural" because we cannot "imagine 'good' as existing *by itself* in time" supports this conclusion. It is unclear, in other words, in what way the "non-naturalness" of goodness is related to Moore's strict claim that

> 'good' is indefinable,' and... to deny it involves a fallacy... capable of strict proof: for to deny it involves contradictions.[10]

Significantly, then, there appears to be a striking ambivalence in the argument of the first two chapters of *Principia Ethica* which suggests to me that Moore himself is unaware of the two different lines of thought or two different senses of the naturalistic fallacy implicit in the "first step" of his general argument. The whole problem, I suggest further, finds its source in Moore's thinking early in Chapter I, where he says,

> My business is solely with that *object or idea,* which I hold, rightly or wrongly, that the word is generally used to stand for. What I want to discover is the nature of that object or idea.[11] (Italics mine)

Moore's language here and elsewhere in Chapter I certainly would lead us to believe that the phrase "object or idea" is unproblematic. But the difference between goodness as a property of things and goodness as an idea is significant and leads to a crucial shift in Moore's argument. In fact, it is the very shift in Moore's thinking and argument between Chapters I and II to which we have been referring above. Consequently, recognizing this shift in Moore's thought should not only clarify for us the relationship that Moore's "anti-naturalism" or "non-naturalism" has to the important first chapter of *Principia Ethica,* but should clarify as well much that is obscure in Chapter I itself. In brief, if it turns out that the arguments in Chapters I and II are logically independent, the argument in Chapter II might well suggest to us a new and more fruitful direction into which our analysis of Chapter I can take.

Goodness: Object or Idea?

George C. Kerner points to this same question about Moore's argument in Chapter I in his book, *The Revolution in Ethical Theory,* when he says,

> In Moore's own work the difference between ideas and properties or attributes is blurred. Perhaps his phrase "object or idea" merely provides stylistic variety. We need not try to decide this issue. It is plain that Moore was a "Platonist", that for him the word 'good' stood for an entity of some sort and that according to him it was the simple and unanalyzable nature of that entity that made the term 'good' indefinable. It is Moore's "Platonism" and his belief in the ultimate simplicity of goodness as a kind of entity that has made his view outdated and unpalatable to many.[12]

But Professor Kerner goes on to discount any value in pursuing this difference, because, in his words,

> We shall see eventually that there are considerable portions of Moore's doctrine that can be interpreted without any reference to goodness as an entity.[13]

Perhaps, however, it is *because* Professor Kerner ignores those "portions of Moore's doctrine that (cannot) be interpreted without any reference to good as an entity," i.e. the major argument of Chapter II and the line of thought of Chapter I which it reflects, that allows, or leads, him to conclude, with so many others, that

> (Moore's) Open Question Argument, although it does not demonstrate the impossibility of a naturalistic approach in ethics in principle, does constitute a powerful weapon against all the known varieties of naturalism. In one form or another this argument has been used to point out basic difficulties in all existing naturalistic systems.[14]

We ought, therefore, to take a second look at the "naturalistic fallacy," and the Open Question Argument underlying it, of Chapter I, determining, if we can, why Moore sometimes speaks of goodness as a property of things, and sometimes as a notion or idea. If it turns out that Moore's view of goodness as an "object," his "Platonism," as Professor Kerner refers to it, is intimately connected, in his own thinking, at least, with his "non-naturalism," then it should prove quite valuable to identify and evaluate this connection. After all, it would strike me as rather extraordinary that a "powerful weapon against all the known varieties of naturalism" could grow out of a weak and faulty foundation. For, as I will attempt to show, Moore's "non-naturalism," as well as his "anti-naturalism," is rooted in his "Platonism," his view of goodness as an object *in rerum natura,* and that this view in turn is rooted in his theory of definition in Chapter I. In brief, my position is that just as the argument of Chapter I leads us to Moore's theory of definition for its source and support, so also does the argument of Chapter II. That just as the inapplicability of Moore's theory of definition to natural objects renders his "anti-naturalism" invalid, so do other weaknesses in that theory render his "non-naturalism" invalid. But finally, and most significantly, just as Moore's thinking on the nature and role of definition in ethics leads ultimately to his "naturalistic fallacy" and non-naturalism," so too does Hume's thinking on what is essentially the same theory of definition reflect his "naturalism" and his view that goodness is not a specific thing—neither a specific object nor a specific notion nor even a specific set of values. My view is, then, that it is Moore's rather remarkable misunderstanding and misapplication of a theory of definition held by Hume, himself, among others, which gives birth in *Principia Ethica* to the views that naturalistic ethics rests on a fundamental mistake and that goodness is a simple "non-natural" object.

Moore's Theory of Definition and
Its Relationship to the Strict Sense of the Naturalistic Fallacy

Clearly, the view that every complex whole is ultimately composed of absolutely simple things is the major presupposition of Moore's thought in Chapter I. But his many problems and confusions arise not so much from this general metaphysical position as from what he mistakenly infers from it. Moore appears to believe that if every complex whole is ultimately composed of absolutely simple terms or parts, then (a) "the most important sense of definition" is the enumeration of those terms or parts, (b) the simple terms or parts are consequently themselves not susceptible to "real" analysis or definition, and (c) whatever is not susceptible to "real" analysis or definition, the Open Question Argument constituting the proper test, is consequently absolutely simple in reality, i.e. its true or real nature is absolutely simple. The combination of (a), (b), and (c) constitutes the strict sense of the naturalistic fallacy, the sense in which, in Moore's words,

> We should find we had to hold that an orange was exactly the same thing as a stool, a piece of paper, a lemon, anything you like.[15]

Moreover, this strict (and artless) sense of the "fallacy"gives rise to Moore's brand of "non-naturalism," as it entails the view that goodness is an object *in rerum natura* with which nothing can or ought to be identified. It is a short step from (a) or (b), from Moore's theory of definition to the conclusion that there are necessarily *terms* which are indefinable. This much is made quite explicit in Chapter I:

> And so it is with all objects, not previously known, which we are able to define: they are all complex; all composed of parts, which may themselves, in the first instance, be capable of similar definition, but which must in the end be reducible to simplest parts, which can no longer be defined. But yellow and good, we say, are not complex: they are notions of that simple kind, out of which definitions are composed and with which the power of further defining ceases.[16]

But how does Moore arrive at (c), the position that what can be shown to be indefinable "in the most important sense of definition" is by virtue of that fact an absolutely simple thing in reality? What, in other words, is the connection between the view that significant definition is the enumeration of the simplest terms of a concept or notion and the view that things or objects are composed of simplest parts, or more simply, between the terms "simplest notion" and "simplest part"? Our problem, then, is to explain the relationship in Moore's thinking that (c) has to (a) and (b).

Moore is apparently working under the assumption that the theory of definition, which he briefly, but confidently, formulates in Chapter I, is merely a rough re-statement of a widely accepted theory of "real" definition. Leibniz gives clear expression to this view of definition and analysis and the mechanistic view of nature which supports it:

> Now since the wisdom of God has always been recognized in the details of the mechanical structures of certain particular bodies, it should also be shown in the general economy of the world and in the constitution of the laws of nature. . . [Thus] When at length everything which enters into a definition or into distinct knowledge is known distinctly, even back to the primitive conception, I call that knowledge adequate. When my mind understands at once and distinctly all the primitive ingredients of a conception, then we have intuitive knowledge.[17]

While Hume says,

> Complex ideas may, perhaps, be well known by definition, which is nothing but an enumeration of those parts or simple ideas that compose them.[18]

And indeed, on a merely verbal level, Moore's position is essentially similar to this traditional theory of "real" definition, as the following statement bears out: According to Moore,

> The most important sense of 'definition' is that in which a definition states what are the parts which invariably compose a certain whole. . .[19]

But on a closer analysis, crucial differences between these three positions are disclosed, and it is Moore's own peculiar (mis)understanding of the "composition theory" which guides his thinking, and ultimately creates too many problems, in Chapters I and II.

First of all, Moore and Leibniz agree that everything, i.e. substances, physical or otherwise, in the world are either simple or composed of simples. But Leibniz does not, like Moore, believe that "simple substances," i.e. substances which have no parts, are unanalyzable or indefinable. In fact, a prominent instance of the analysis and definition of "absolute simples" is Leibniz's treatment of his "monads." But the "atoms" of Democritus and. Lucretius serve equally well as examples. And our own "atoms" were analyzed far before we had found any "parts." But a less abstract example, that of a color, something which admittedly has no parts, is given by Hume. He says,

> Thus when a globe of white marble is presented, we receive only the impression of a white colour dispos'd in a certain form, nor are we able to separate and distinguish the colour from the form. But observing afterwards a globe of black marble and a cube of white, and comparing them with our former object, we find two separate

41

resemblances, in what formerly seem'd, and really is, perfectly inseparable.[20]

The point is simply that even if everything in the world is either a simple substance in virtue of having no parts or is composed of such simple substances, it does not follow, as Moore claims, that when we arrive at an absolute simple, "the power of further definition ceases."[21] The "composition theory" is a useful method of analysis and definition when dealing with wholes which are complex in virtue of having parts. Mechanical objects are composed, and conceived, in terms of their parts. Moore's "chimaera", like most imaginary objects, is conceived in terms of its separable parts—which is precisely why it was such a poor example of "the most important sense of definition." For the greater part of our experience is with "things" or "objects" which are certainly complex, but are not so in virtue of their parts. Our sentiments and emotions are obvious examples. And as we saw in Chapter I, the thorough application of the "composition theory" of definition to any "natural object" is ultimately fruitless. In short, it is just as foolish to believe that because something is simple (in Moore's sense) that it has no properties and qualities, as to believe that (in Moore's sense)

> You can give a definition of a horse, because a horse has many different properties and qualities, all of which you can enumerate.[22]

And once it is recognized that both these claims underlie the Open Argument, it should become clear that argument does not "constitute a powerful weapon against all known varieties of naturalism."[23]

The Two Senses of the Naturalistic Fallacy and the Shift in Moore's Argument

Once it is recognized that it is Moore's thinking on definition which leads him to the view that goodness is an object and to confuse this object with anything else is to commit a strict and simple fallacy, one can understand the significance of the chosen motto of *Principia Ethica*, "Everything is what it is, and not another thing."[24] Often in Chapter I, however, Moore seems to mean by the naturalistic fallacy just this sort of trivial mistake. Let me quote a passage at length, which clearly shows the significance that Bishop Butler's maxim carries for Moore. He says,

> It is a very simple fallacy indeed. When we say that an orange is yellow, we do not think our statement binds us to hold that 'orange' means nothing else than 'yellow,' or that nothing can be yellow but an orange. Supposing the orange is also sweet! Does that bind us to say that 'sweet' is exactly the same thing as 'yellow,' that 'sweet' must be defined as 'yellow'? And supposing it be recognized that 'yellow' just means 'yellow' and nothing else whatever, does that make it any more difficult to hold that oranges are yellow? Most certainly it does not: on the contrary, it would be absolutely meaningless to say that oranges were yellow, unless yellow did in the end mean just 'yellow' and nothing else whatever—unless it was absolutely indefinable. We should not get any very clear notion about things, which are yellow—we should not get

42

very far with our science, is we were bound to hold that every-thing which was yellow, *meant* exactly the same thing as yellow.[25]

The fallacy is simple indeed. If anyone ever confused the sweetness with the yellowness of an orange simply because they are constantly conjoined or confused the orange with one or both of them, he would certainly be guilty of a fallacy. But I do not believe that it warrants any special name; one should simply identify it as a simpleminded confusion or a gross misuse of language or a perceptual absurdity or by some other more appropriate human malfunction. But I cannot myself imagine the circumstances under which such a mistake could occur. Citing as an example that we might mistakenly take the sweetness of an orange to mean "exactly the same thing" as the yellowness of an orange, does not help us in the least. The naturalistic fallacy in this sense is too trivial and uninteresting to bother with—and in fact, Moore does not bother with it in this sense except for a brief space in Chapter I. For there he is concerned to show that the naturalistic fallacy is a strict fallacy; he is not concerned to show there, as he is later, that it is also a fallacy with actual instances, that Mill, Bentham, Sidgwick, and others, actually committed it. For this purpose, Moore shifts to a more plausible sense of the fallacy. And it is obviously around this second sense of the fallacy that the real issues lie.

The basic difference between these two senses of the naturalistic fallacy centers on Moore's mistaken belief that analysis by enumeration of simplest terms discloses the "real" nature of things and that consequently our "simplest notions" correspond to "simplest things"—properties and qualities—in reality. If Moore had recognized, like Hume, that many of our most complex notions are representative of what is in reality quite indivisible in respect to its parts, and *vice versa,* he might well have recognized the inapplicability of the "composition theory of definition" to moral phenomena and consequently, the fundamental distinctiveness of the content of moral experience. Indeed, the wisdom of the *Treatise* is nowhere more evident than in Books II and III, where Hume ignores the rigid framework of the "composition theory" of definition (and associationist psychology) in dealing with moral experience. For although he emphasizes throughout Book I that "ideas" and "impressions" are identical in all respects save liveliness and that the principles of analysis there are applicable to moral experience, Hume says this in Book II,

> Ideas may be compar'd to the extension and solidity of matter, and impressions, especially reflective ones, to colours, tastes, smells and other sensible qualities. Ideas never admit of a total union, but are endow'd with a kind of impenetrability, by which they exclude each other, and are capable of forming a compound by their conjunction, not by their mixture. On the other hand, impressions and passions are susceptible of an entire union; and like colours, *may be blended so perfectly together, that each of them may lose itself, and contribute only to vary that uniform impression,* which arises from the whole.[26] (Italics mine)

In other words, not only are ideas and impressions *not* identical in every respect save liveliness, but they are positively so different that definition by an enumeration of parts is inapplicable to them, since "impressions" are comparable to "colours, tastes, smells and other sensible qualities," which "may be blended so perfectly together, that each of them may lose itself, and contribute only to vary that uniform impression. . ."

Understanding this distinction between moral experience and other types of experience, or between "ideas" and "impressions" in Hume's terms, is preliminary to understanding Hume's answer to the fundamental questions of moral enquiry. In this respect, for Hume the basic questions of moral enquiry resolve themselves into the following:

> Now as perceptions resolve themselves into two kinds, viz. *impressions* and *ideas,* this distinction gives rise to a question, with which we shall open up our present enquiry concerning morals, *whether 'tis by means of our* ideas *or* impressions *we distinguish betwixt vice and virtue, and pronounce an action blameable or praiseworthy?* This will immediately cut off all loose discourses and declamations, and reduce us to something precise and exact on the present subject.[27]

And his answer is,

> 'Twas therefore a concern for our own, and the publick interest, which made us establish the laws of justice; and nothing can be more certain, than that it is not any relation of ideas, which gives us this concern, but our impressions and sentiments, without which every thing in nature is perfectly indifferent to us, and can never in the least affect us. The sense of justice, therefore, is not founded on our ideas, but on our impressions.[28]

And equally, our sense of *goodness* "is not founded on our ideas, but on our impressions." And since our "impressions and passions are susceptible of an entire union; and like colours, may be blended so perfectly together, that each of them may lose itself. . ."[29] definition by an enumeration of parts is inapplicable to moral enquiry.

Conclusion

Hume's moral theory will be considered further in the next chapter. Our brief discussion of his views above, however, should suffice to allow us to draw our final conclusions concerning Moore's criticism of "naturalistic ethics." For although Hume does not explicitly formulate a theory of definition other than the "composition theory," it is clear, as I attempt to show in the next chapter, that Hume employs an alternative method of analysis and definition in moral enquiry. We need only recognize at this point that the object of definition and analysis in moral enquiry for Hume is not the exhaustive enumeration of simples entailed by the "composition theory," but the more reasonable and plausible task of identifying those properties of a concept which distinguish it from all other concepts.

Significantly, then, if Moore had recognized this comparatively modest goal of definition, he might have altered his ethical position in a number of fundamental ways. Instead of viewing his Open Question Argument as a club with which to enforce the "naturalistic fallacy" and, consequently, to pommel "naturalistic ethics," Moore might have viewed it as a tool for understanding and evaluating the substantive claims of other ethical theories—as opposed to a tool for evaluating supposed definitions of goodness. For in view of the above stated role of definition, the object of the Open Question Argument, i.e. of asking oneself whether in fact one has a unique object before one's mind when reflecting on the concept of goodness, would be to determine whether, to one's reflective judgment, there is a unique property or characteristic of goodness. And if it were to turn out, as it does for Mill, for example, that pleasure seems always to be characteristic of the concept of goodness when we reflect upon it, then we would be justified in *defining* goodness in terms of pleasure—meaning not that goodness and pleasure are identical in every respect, that pleasure is "absolutely and entirely the same with goodness,"[30] but that pleasure is a distinguishing characteristic of goodness.

In this respect, were Mill or anyone else guilty of a fallacy, it would not be the strict one of confusing an absolute simple with what it is not or a whole with what is only a part of it, but a simple matter of mistaken judgment of *fact,* viz. whether to our reflective judgment pleasure, or whatever, is invariably recognized to be a characteristic of goodness. In his convincing defense of Mill against Moore's criticisms, Everett Hall contrasts Mill's position with Moore's on precisely this point:

> To an empiricist who eschews all intuitive self-evidence, no ethical first principle can be strictly proved. All that one can do is to present considerations that will lead honest and reasonable people to accept such a principle. These considerations, for an empiricist, must turn on what people actually desire.

> . . . the self-evidence of a first principle takes us outside the system. But that brings up the serious question of how a whole ethical system can be established, a question that such an intuitionist as Moore never clearly faced just because he never saw this ambiguity in the concept of self-evidence.[31]

And indeed, this seems clearly to be the import of Mill's famous passage in his *Utilitarianism.* He says,

> It has already been remarked that questions of ultimate ends do not admit of proof, in the ordinary acceptation of the term. To be incapable of proof by reasoning is common to all first principles: to the first premises of our knowledge as well as to those of our conduct. But the former, being matters of fact, may be the subject of a direct appeal to the faculties which judge of fact—namely, our senses, and *our internal consciousness.*[32] (Italics mine)

Mill is pointing out, in fundamental disagreement with Moore, that questions of knowledge are different from questions of conduct in virtue of the fact that the former can be settled or determined by direct perception, by "direct appeal to. . . our internal consciousness," while the latter cannot. In respect to conduct,

> ...the morality of an individual action is not a question of direct perception, but of the application of a law to an individual case.[33]

The question that Mill faces, then, is the question: How can one establish his ethical first principle without appealing directly to "our internal consciousness" or "reflective judgment," to use Moore's terminology. This is a problem, as Everett Hall has pointed out, that Moore never faces, since Moore does appeal directly to our "reflective judgment," resting his case on a mysterious form of "direct perception" or "self-evidence," which he labels "intuition."[34] Had Moore recognized Mill's problem, and indeed the problem facing any ethical naturalist, then he would have realized as well, I am certain, that Mill is not attempting a "proof" of his ethical first principle, but only trying to make it acceptable to reasonable men.

Consequently, there is not the least suggestion in Mill's argument of the sort of definition of which Moore is speaking and therefore of the sort of strict fallacy, which he labels the "naturalistic fallacy." That Moore is fundamentally in error as to Mill's purpose, and as to the purpose of definition in ethics, may be further disclosed by considering what Moore confidently, but mistakenly believes he is proving by his critique of "naturalistic ethics." He says,

> In this second division of my subject. . . I have hitherto only tried to establish one definite result, and that a negative one: namely that pleasure is not the sole good. This result, if true, refutes half, or more than half, of the ethical theories which have ever been held, and is, therefore, not without importance.[35]

If Moore had only seen that Mill is not trying to show that pleasure is the sole good, but rather, that it is the only general fact in our experience which can serve as evidence for what is the sole good, then he might well have disputed with Mill, but for reasons much different from those afforded by his framework of verbal stipulations on the nature of definition and the subject-matter of ethics.

Our conclusion, then, is that Moore's "naturalistic fallacy," interpreted in the strict sense as a specific fallacy, is nothing more than an extension to ethical theory of his mistaken conception of the role and nature of definition. And that consequently, since Moore's "non-naturalism" presupposes the validity of his theory of definition, the two major theses of *Principia Ethica* can now be rejected. But rather than showing that Moore's position in ethics is false, my primary intention from the beginning has been to show that Moore's mistaken thinking on ethical theory has led him, and subsequently others, to misunderstand and misinterpret previous ethical theories. My purpose in this is not only to correct what has become a widespread historical injustice, but to provide a more reasonable and receptive philosophical environment in which the "naturalists" of the 18th and 19th centuries can be read and evaluated. I have tried to exhibit this misunderstanding in a general fashion in the case of Mill's *Utilitarianism,* and I hope to show it in greater detail in the next chapter where we consider Hume's ethics.

[1] *International Journal of Ethics,* 1903, p. 116.

[2] *Principia,* p. 14.

[3] *Ibid.,* pp. 39-40.

[4] *Ibid.,* p. 41.

[5] *Ibid.,* p. 41.

[6] Carl Wellman, *The Language of Ethics,* Cambridge, Harvard University Press, 1961, p. 47.

[7] *Principia,* p. 41.

[8] Cf. pp. 22-23 above.

[9] *Principia,* p. 144.

[10] *Ibid.,* p. 77.

[11] *Ibid.,* p. 6.

[12] George Kerner, *The Revolution in Ethical Theory,* New York, Oxford University Press, 1966, p. 8.

[13] *Ibid.,* p. 8.

[14] George Kerner, *The Revolution in Ethical Theory,* New York, Oxford University Press, 1966, p. 40.

[15] *Principia,* p. 14.

[16] *Ibid.,* pp. 7-8.

[17] Gottfried Wilhelm Freiherr von Leibniz, *Knowledge and Metaphysics,* in *Leibniz,* ed. by Philip P. Wiener, New York, Charles Scribner's Sons, 1951, pp. 320-325.

[18] David Hume, *Enquiry Concerning the Human Understanding,* La Salle, Illinois, Open Court Publishing Co., 1966, p. 66.

[19] *Principia,* p. 9.

[20] *Treatise,* p. 25.

[21] *Principia,* p. 8.

[22] *Ibid.,* p. 8.

[23] George Kerner, *The Revolution in Ethical Theory,* New York, Oxford University Press, 1966, p. 40.

[24] According to Moore, these are the words of Bishop Butler.

[25] *Principia,* p. 14.

[26] *Treatise,* p. 366.

[27] *Ibid.,* p. 456.

[28] *Ibid.,* p. 496.

[29] *Ibid.,* p. 366.

[30] *Principia,* p. 10.

[31] Everett Hall, "The 'Proof' of Utility in Bentham and Mill," in *Categorical Analysis,* ed. by E. M. Adams, Chapel Hill, The University of North Carolina

Press, 1964, pp. 122-123.

[32]John Stuart Mill, *Utilitarianism,* in *The English Philosopher From Bacon to Mill,* ed. by Edwin A. Burtt, New York, Modern Library, 1939, p. 923.

[33]*Ibid.,* p. 896.

[34]*Principia,* pp. 143-144.

[35]*Ibid.,* pp. 145-146. It is noteworthy that Moore, unlike many of his followers, feels obliged to prove independently of his "first division" (the argument in Chapter I) that the general principle that "pleasure is the sole good" is false. The clear suggestion in Chapter I is that the argument there, viz. that goodness is simple and indefinable, *is proof* that "pleasure is not the sole good." In other words, the direction and tone of the "second division" of *Principia Ethica* appear to substantiate what I am here arguing, namely, that Moore and Mill are in factual disagreement, rather than a fundamental methodological one.

CHAPTER THREE

Introduction

I have attempted to show in the first two chapters of this work that the major claims of *Principia Ethica*—that all or most ethical theories rest on a common mistake and that goodness is a simple, unanalyzable, non-natural property or quality—fail to withstand philosophical scrutiny. The former claim, the "naturalistic fallacy," as Moore labels it, takes the form of the Open Question Argument in Chapter I of *Principia Ethica*. My basic criticism of this argument was that it rests upon a mistaken and irrelevant theory of definition: mistaken in virtue of its failure to satisfy Moore's requirement that all significant definition disclose the "real" nature of things, and irrelevant in virtue of its exclusion of the possibility of ever defining "natural" objects in the first place. Consequently, we concluded that Moore's theory of definition is not "the most important sense of definition" in ethics; more importantly, by resting upon a view of definition which is inappropriate to the content of naturalistic ethical theories, his crucial Open Question Argument prejudges the case against them.

In contrast with the negative posture of Chapter I, the "naturalistic fallacy" takes the form of a positive, substantive claim in Chapter II of *Principia Ethica* to the effect that goodness is a "non-natural" property or quality and that consequently any theory which identifies goodness with "natural" properties and qualities is basically in error. I have attempted to show that Moore's non-naturalism or "Platonism," as Professor Kerner refers to it, rests as well upon the theory of definition espoused in Chapter I. Irrespective, then, of Moore's obscure argument in Chapter II purporting to prove the non-natural nature of goodness, we have good grounds for rejecting both the positive and negative claims of *Principia Ethica* in virtue of their direct dependence upon a mistaken and irrelevant theory of definition.

These, then, are the technical conclusions of our analysis and evaluation of the major claims of *Principia Ethica.* But left as such, they carry little more than technical significance. The major purpose of my criticism has been rather to clear the air for the more important task of providing an unprejudiced introduction to "naturalistic ethics," those theories, as Moore expresses it, which view value in terms of "what is admittedly an object of experience."[1] I wish to attempt now to show in what ways our criticism of Moore's "naturalistic fallacy" and our discussion of the nature of definition suggest answers to the broader questions concerning the nature of ethical theory and the ground of morality itself, issues on which the question of the correctness and value of "naturalistic ethics" ultimately rests.

We saw, for example, that Moore's view of definition in ethics is intimately connected with his view that a fundamental error is common to most ethical theories and that goodness is simple, indefinable, and unanalyzable. So also are these latter views quite naturally connected with broader questions of ethical value and theory, and it is perhaps Moore's position on these issues that provides the seed of his misunderstanding of "naturalistic ethics." I would argue that there is this close connection between Moore's positive approach to ethical theory and his negative misunderstanding of "naturalistic ethics," and that the best way to exhibit and evaluate this connection in Moore's thinking is to compare his position with that of a representative "naturalist." Specifically, I believe that an understanding of Hume's position on these issues will provide both an explanation of why Moore sees "naturalistic ethical theories" as resting on a fundamental error and a comprehensive answer to Moore's basic objections to them.

Hume's "composition theory of definition" and Moore's preliminary misunderstanding

I do not wish to suggest that Moore consciously prejudges the case against "naturalistic ethical theories," or against Hume's ethical theory in particular. Moore appears to be genuinely confident of the philosophical soundness and fairness of his theory of definition. Moreover, his confidence is not without historical justification. Hume, interestingly enough, espouses a theory of definition in Book I of the *Treatise* which is similar to the theory of "real" definition of Chapter I of *Principia Ethica.* It is not surprising, then, that Moore fails to question its relevance to "naturalistic ethical theories." But Books II and III of the *Treatise* can be distinguished from Book I in a number of fundamental ways, not the least of which is in their distinctive conceptual and methodological demands. And it is precisely this conceptual and methodological distinction which Moore fails to draw, and by failing to do so, I suggest, produces himself the substance of his famous "fallacy."

When Hume says that the natural sentiments, because simple, can never be defined by "a multitude of words"[2] and Moore says that good can never be defined because it has no parts,[3] they both imply that there is a type of definition which is only appropriate to complex notions. James Gibson entitles this general view of analysis and definition the "composition theory," and he presents us with a good brief view of its background and appeal for post-Newtonian philosophers. He says,

> For thinkers of the seventeenth century, to whom all ideas of development were entirely foreign, the place which is now filled by the conception of evolution was occupied by the idea of composition, with the implied distinction between the simple and the complex. A complex whole being regarded as the mere sum of its constituent parts, these latter were not thought to undergo any modification as the result of their combination; similarly, the whole was supposed to be directly resolvable into its parts without remainder. . . To comprehend a complex whole all that was required was a process of direct analysis by which the simples contained in it were distinguished. Then, starting with the simples, thought could retrace with perfect adequacy, the process by which the whole had originally been constituted. . . It was for this reason that the question of the determination of the logical content of our ideas came to be so closely connected in Locke's mind with an investigation of their origin and manner of formation.[4]

It is for a similar reason that the question of the determination of the logical content of our ideas came to be so closely connected in Hume's mind with an investigation of their origin and manner of formation. Indeed, the "composition theory" of analysis and definition follows directly from Hume's critical principle to the effect that simple ideas exactly correspond to simple impressions. "Ideas always represent their objects or impressions."[5]

> If it be a compound idea, it must arise from compound impressions. If simple, from simple impressions.[6]

If, then, impressions give rise to ideas and since we use words to stand for ideas,[7] we can test the legitimacy of a simple idea by producing the simple impression and of a complex idea by first employing the "composition" or "enumerative" method of analysis and then by producing the respective simple impressions. Hume explicitly supports this view in the *Enquiry Concerning the Human Understanding*. He says there,

> It seems a proposition, which will not admit of much dispute, that all our ideas are nothing but copies of our impressions, or, in other words, that it is impossible for us to think of any thing, which we have not antecedently felt, either by our external or internal senses. I have endeavoured to explain and prove this proposition, and have expressed my hopes, that, by a proper application of it, men

51

may reach a greater clearness and precision in philosophical reasonings, than what they have hitherto been able to attain. Complex ideas may, perhaps, be well known by definition, which is nothing but an enumeration of those parts or simple ideas, that compose them. But when we have pushed up definitions to the most simple ideas, and find still some ambiguity and obscurity; what resources are we then possessed of? By what invention can we throw light upon these ideas, and render them altogether precise and determinate to our intellectual view? Produce the impressions or original sentiments, from which the ideas are copied.[8]

When we entertain, therefore, any suspicion that a term is employed without any meaning or idea (as is but too frequent), we need but enquire, *from what impression is that supposed idea derived?*[9]

Once we unfold the methodological implications of Hume's "composition theory," a rather remarkable and surprising conclusion suggests itself, namely, that the methodology in Chapter I of *Principia Ethica* is essentially similar to that of Book I of the *Treatise*. More specifically, this is to say that the "naturalistic fallacy" is essentially the claim that the "composition theory" of definition and analysis does not apply to the moral concept "good"—which is to say that the methodology of Book I of the *Treatise* is inapplicable to Book II of the *Treatise*. For, according to Hume, we test the legitimacy, or correctness, of a proposed definition of a complex term first by enumerating the simple parts which compose it, secondly by finding the simple impressions which give rise to the simple ideas, and finally by comparing this latter sum with the original complex idea. If the comparison produces an identity, then the definition is correct. This is precisely Moore's procedure, known as the Open Question Argument, in Chapter I of *Principia Ethica*:

We must think just as clearly and correctly about a horse, if we thought of all its parts and their arrangement instead of thinking of the whole: we could, I say, think how a horse differed from a donkey just as well, just as truly, in this way, as now we do, only not so easily; but there is nothing whatsoever which we could so substitute for good; and that is what I mean, when I say that good is indefinable.[10]

Moore, in other words, employs Hume's own theory of definition and analysis as the key critical weapon in his attack on Hume's approach to moral enquiry.

Is Hume, then, guilty of a "fallacy"?

It seems as if we have reached a dilemma. If we accept Hume's theory of definition and analysis, we must accept the substance of Moore's critical position in Chapter I of *Principia Ethica*. At which point, therefore, we would have to reject Hume's approach to moral enquiry. On the other hand, if we reject Hume's position on definition and analysis, even though we would avoid by that the force of the "naturalistic fallacy," we would have good reason for doubting the strength and clarity of Hume's general argument. For Hume does

52

say on a number of occasions that all of the sciences, the social as well as the physical, rest upon the same fundamental principles. Indeed, this is perhaps the main theme of the Introduction to the *Treatise*. Hume says there,

> In pretending therefore to explain the principles of human nature, we in effect propose a complete system of the sciences, built on a foundation almost entirely new, and the only one upon which they can stand with any security.[11]

It is quite natural to assume, therefore, that Hume employs the *same* methodology in his moral enquiry, Books II and III of the *Treatise,* as he does in Book I. But perhaps it is just this assumption, so fundamental to Moore's critical position, which is unjustified.

Hume's method of analysis and definition in moral enquiry.

Norman Kemp Smith points out that

> There are in fact. . . two types of psychology in the *Treatise*—a psychology Hutchesonian in type, and a psychology modelled on analogies drawn from the physical sciences. Upon the former he was constantly to fall back; but it is the latter which alone receives explicit formulation.[12]

For basically similar reasons, I suggest that there are in fact two types of definition and analysis in the *Treatise*—one which is modelled on analogies drawn from the physical sciences, viz. the "composition theory," and one modelled on the facts of moral experience. Though Hume explicitly supports the "composition theory" in Book I of the *Treatise* as constituting the proper account of

> those complex ideas, which are the common subjects of our thoughts and reasoning, and generally arise from some principle of union among our simple ideas,[13]

he nevertheless accounts for the complex notions of moral and political philosophy in a distinctly different manner in Books II and III.

In fact, Hume begins his analysis in Book II, "Of the Passions," by considering the method of definition and analysis most appropriate to the natural passions. He says,

> The passions of PRIDE and HUMILITY being simple and uniform impressions, 'til impossible we can ever, by a multitude of words, give a just definition of them, or indeed of any of the passions.[14]

and later in Book II, he says,

> 'Tis altogether impossible to give any definition of the passions of love and hatred: and that because they produce merely a simple impression, without any mixture or composition.[15]

Hume is here making two points. The first is that we can never give a just definition of a simple notion, i.e. a notion which is not susceptible to part-whole analysis, by means of a verbal definition, "by a multitude of words." This is the same point that Moore is emphasizing in Chapter I of *Principia Ethica* when he says,

> My point is that 'good' is a simple notion, just as 'yellow' is a simple notion: that, just as you cannot, by any manner of means, ex-

plain to any one who does not already know it, what yellow is, so you cannot explain what good is.[16]

But from the obvious fact that the "composition theory" of definition is inappropriate to simple notions, Hume does not draw the conclusion, as does Moore, that simple notions are therefore indefinable. Hume does not, in other words, share Moore's view that the only important sense of definition in moral enquiry is that

> in which a definition states what are the parts which invariably compose a certain whole.[17]

The second point, then, is that we justifiably can and naturally do employ an alternative method of definition in dealing with simple notions. Hume emphasizes this point in the first pages of the *Treatise*. He says there,

> To give a child an idea of scarlet or orange, of sweet or bitter, I present the objects, or in other words, convey to him these impressions: but proceed not so absurdly, as to endeavor to produce the impressions by exciting the ideas.[18]

Hume does not refer to this method of definition by name, but it is clearly what we refer to today as "ostensive definition."

Now since the natural passions or sentiments constitute for Hume the greater part of the subject-matter of moral enquiry and since these cannot be ostensively defined in the direct manner in which observable simple qualities, e.g. yellow, can, the problem peculiar to definition in Book II of the *Treatise* is how to define a passion ostensively. Hume's answer is,

> The utmost we can pretend to is a description of them, by an enumeration of such circumstances, as attend them.[19]

This statement of method is simple and clear; yet, the actual employment of it obviously demands great effort and wisdom. It involves the painstaking attempt to understand and analyze each of the basic human sentiments, their relationships and relative strengths. It is this advice to ethical theorists which Hume gives in the Introduction to the *Treatise*:

> We must therefore glean up our experiments in this science from a cautious observation of human life, and take them as they appear in the common course of the world, by men's behaviour in company, in affairs, and in their pleasures. Where experiments of this kind are judiciously collected and compared, we may hope to establish on them a science, which will not be inferior in certainty, and will be much superior in utility to any other of human comprehension.[20]

Whether or not Hume's particular "psychology," his analyses of human sentiment, is correct or exhaustive is not our main concern. The important point is to recognize the fundamental role that the question of definition plays in determining the ultimate nature of moral enquiry, even at the seemingly neutral level of Book II of the *Treatise*. On the one hand, if we reject Hume's approach to definition in Book II, then we reject, in effect, any philosophical role that the natural sentiments might play in moral enquiry. On the other hand, if we accept Moore's view of definition to the effect that part-whole analysis is the only philosophically acceptable method, then we end up with the same unreasonable restrictions. A rejection of Hume's method or an acceptance of Moore's would, in one step, prejudge the case against Hume and any other attempt to deal philosophically with the natural sentiments.

The question of definition, however, is equally crucial in respect to Book III of the *Treatise*, where Hume attempts to define and analyze such complex moral notions as "goodness" and "justice." Moore's "anti-naturalism," his "naturalistic fallacy," it must be remembered, is based upon the assumption that the only valid way to define a complex notion is by employing the "composition theory" of definition:

> You can give a definition of a horse, because a horse has many different properties and qualities, all of which you can enumerate.[21]

> It is in this sense that I deny good to be definable. I say that it is not composed of any parts, which we can substitute for it in our minds when we are thinking of it. We might think just as clearly and correctly about a horse, if we thought of all its parts and their arrangement instead of thinking of the whole. . . [22]

Now, if Moore's assumption concerning definition and analysis were correct, then we could make two important inferences: first, we could infer that Hume is attempting to state, in Book III, "the parts which invariably compose" justice and goodness. And secondly, we could assume that the legitimate test of the correctness of Hume's definitions would be to judge whether or not

> We might think just as clearly and correctly about (justice or goodness), if we thought of all its parts and their arrangement instead of thinking of the whole. . .[23]

We could assume, in other words, the legitimacy and appropriateness of the Open Question Argument.

Moore's assumption, however, is unjustified and false in both directions. Hume is not concerned to find the one "correct" verbal definition of goodness, or justice, or, indeed, of any other moral concept. I am not certain what sense, if any, such an attempt would carry for Hume. Such an attempt would presuppose, I imagine, that complex concepts such as justice stand for some set of characteristics and qualities, which are not only in a definite, static relationship, but which are each verbally and conceptually identifiable. That Hume would not accept such a view of complex moral notions, however much evidence to the contrary Book I of the *Treatise* suggests, should be clear from the mere fact that for Hume the natural sentiments play a fundamental role in all moral thought and action. Once we acknowledge this possiblility, which we must, if we are not to prejudge the case against Hume, then we should recognize that a moral concept such as "justice" is neither a static complex of particulars nor susceptible to the verbal and conceptual identification demanded by the Open Question Argument. You cannot, in short, give a definition of "justice," or "goodness," in terms of its parts, even though it does have many different properties and qualities, many of which you can in fact enumerate, because you can never enumerate *all* its different properties and qualities. The point is that, even if one were to enumerate all the known or suspected properties or qualities or "parts" of "justice," for example, that he or anyone else in the world had ever considered, it would still *not* be possible to *know* that one had been exhaustive. Quite similarly, it would never be possible for us to know that we had exhaustively enumerated all the parts of the atom, for example, even though it is possible to exhaust all present knowledge in the form of an enumerative definition. It is not surprising then that Moore, who holds a quasi atomic theory of reality, i.e. that *absolute* natural particulars can be identified, should think that all natural objects were so reducible and identifiable. But you cannot think just as clearly and correctly about "justice," or "goodness," by thinking of all its parts and their arrangement instead of thinking of the whole. You simply can never exhaustively enumerate the properties and qualities of a *natural* object. Moore's Open Question Argument is not the proper or relevant test of the correctness of a proposed definition of a concept such as "justice," or "goodness."

An Objection

Analyses of "justice" and "goodness" will be offered in Chapter V, where Hume's "naturalistic" approach is exhibited in relation to Moore's "intuitive," linguistic approach. At this point, an interesting objection might be raised against my view that Moore mistakenly assumes that the factors or "parts" which together constitute our complex moral notions "compose" those concepts in a purely mechanical manner. It could be objected that since my view implies an awareness and recognition on Hume's part of the inapplicability of the "composition theory" to organic, or dynamic, concepts, that Hume's concept and analysis of the "self" suggests a contradiction. However, this objection really affords further evidence for my view that the distinction between Book I, on the one hand, and Books II and III of the *Treatise,* on the other, is methodological, as well as substantive.[24]

Hume does say in the well-known section vi, "Of Personal Identity," of Book I,

For my part, when I enter most intimately into what I call *myself,* I always stumble on some particular perception or other, of heat or cold, light or shade, love or hatred. . . [25]

(Identity is) nothing but a bundle or collection of different perceptions, which succeed each other with an inconceivable rapidity, and are in a perpetual flux and movement.[26]

'Tis evident, that the identity, which we attribute to the human mind, however perfect we may imagine it to be, is not able to run the several different perceptions into one, and make them lose their characters of distinction and difference, which are essential to them. 'Tis still true, that every distinct perception, which enters into the composition of the mind, is a distinct existence, and is different, and distinguishable, and separable from every other perception. . . [27]

But when we compare this view of the "self" with some of the characteristic statements of Books II and III, we are forced to recognize the marked degree to which the mechanical, or Newtonian, scheme of Book I and the "naturalistic," moral approach of Books II and III are incompatible:

'Tis evident, that the idea, or rather impression of ourselves is always intimately present with us, and that our consciousness gives us so lively a conception of our own person, that 'tis not possible to imagine that any thing can in this particular go beyond it.[28]

The idea of ourselves is always intimately present to us, and conveys a sensible degree of vivacity to the idea of any other object, to which we are related. . . The great propensity men have to pride may be consider'd as another phaenomenon.[29]

As the immediate *object* of pride and humility is self or that identical person, of whose thoughts, actions, and sensations we are intimately conscious: so the *object* of love and hatred is some other person, of whose thoughts, actions, and sensations we are not conscious. This is. . .evident from experience.[30]

Though the "self" may indeed be a product of a series, or "bundle," of distinct particulars, what we *mean* and recognize *conceptually* and *verbally* by "self" is something quite distinct from those particulars considered enumeratively. Whatever, then, are the laws of composition which validly pertain to the formation of the "self," they are fundamentally different from the mechanical laws on which the "composition theory" is based.[31]

An equally significant instance of the theoretical and methodological modification that takes place between Books I and Books II and III of the *Treatise* concerns Hume's theory of perception. Of fundamental importance to Hume's epistemological position in Book I are four contentions: (1) that all perceptions can be divided into either "impressions" or "ideas"; (2) that impressions are "original existences" and causally determine ideas; (3) that every idea is an exact copy of the impression which causes or corresponds to it; and (4) that the criterion for determining whether a perception is an impression or idea is "degree of liveliness." (1) and (2) are so basic to Hume's philosophical position as to remain seemingly unchanged and unquestioned throughout the *Treatise*. Yet if we observe the significant modifications which take place in (3) and (4) as the subject matter changes from questions of epistemology to those of morality, we will recognize as well the need for significant qualifications in (1) and (2).

In Book I Hume is quite confident of the fundamental correctness of (3) and (4):

The first circumstance, that strikes my eye, is the great resemblance betwixt our impressions and ideas in every other particular, except their degree of force and vivacity.[32]

That idea of red, which we form in the dark, and that impression, which strikes our eyes in sunshine, differ only in degree, not in nature.[33]

Of (3), however, Hume offers only an indirect proof. He challenges the critic to produce a contrary instance:

> If he does not answer this challenge, as 'tis certain he cannot, we may from his silence and our own observation establish our conclusion.[34]

The proof of (4) is likewise indirect, but it rests upon an assumption which lies at the heart of Book I and which links that book so intimately with Moore's position in *Principia Ethica*. Hume maintains that simple impressions admit of no inner distinction or separation:

> Simple perceptions or impressions and ideas are such as admit of no distinction nor separation. The complex are the contrary to these, and may be distinguished into parts.[35]

These simple impressions of Book I correspond to Moore's "notions of that simple kind, out of which definitions are composed and with which the power of further defining ceases."[36] They are absolute simples, and it would seem reasonable to assume that if such atomic elements constitute the content of immediate experience that there are correspondent ideas which are exact copies of these. And Hume, like Moore, takes an important next step. He goes on to maintain that complex ideas are reducible without remainder to the simple ideas which compose them. And this position is dependent upon the assumption that simple ideas do not undergo alterations in the process of combining to form complex ideas. The ultimate implication of this view together with the view that ideas resemble impressions in every particular except vivacity is that complex ideas are reducible to simple impressions.

> Thus we find, that all simple ideas and impressions resemble each other; and as the complex are formed from them, we may affirm in general, that these two species of perception are exactly correspondent.[37]

No further assumptions or premises are required to justify the theory of definition and the basic methodological procedure of Hume's epistemology:

> Complex ideas may, perhaps, be well known by definition, which is nothing but an enumeration of those parts or simple ideas, that compose them. But when we have pushed up definitions to the most simple ideas, and find still some ambiguity and obscurity; what resources are we then possessed of? By what invention can we throw light upon these ideas, and render them altogether precise and determinate to our intellectual view? *Produce the impressions or original sentiments, from which the ideas are copied.*[38]

And this view, as we have seen, is exactly that of Moore in Chapter I of *Principia Ethica*. Consequently, if Hume's naturalism is to avoid the very errors of its chief critic, it is imperative that Books II and III be distinguished from the basic epistemological assumptions of Book I.

And, indeed, in Book II where Hume is faced with the analysis of human passion or sentiment, he expressly qualifies the above view. Human sentiments, like other impressions of perception, are original existences, simple facts of experience, admitting of no inner distinction or separation. Yet Hume admits a crucial difference between the simple passions and the simple impressions of the understanding. He says,

> Ideas may be compar'd to the extension and solidity of matter, and impressions, especially reflective ones, to colours, tastes, smells and other sensible qualities. Ideas never admit of a total union, but are endow'd with a kind of impenetrability, by which they exclude each other, and are capable of forming a compound by their *conjunction, not by their mixture.* On the other hand, impressions and passions are susceptible of an entire union; and like colours, may be blended so perfectly together, that each of them may lose itself, and contribute only to vary that uniform impression, which arises from the whole. Some of the most curious phenomena of the human mind are deriv'd from this property of the passions.[39]

Hume is saying here that in respect to the passions complex ideas are no longer resolvable into their simplest parts, i.e. that complex ideas are not susceptible to part-whole analysis if those parts are simple passions. Unlike the simple ideas of the understanding which "never admit of a total union, but are endow'd with a kind of impenetrability, by which they exclude each other," the simple passions "are susceptible of an entire union and. . .may be blended so perfectly together, that each of them may lose itself, and contribute only to vary that uniform impression, which arises from the whole." Complex moral ideas, then, do not admit of part-whole analysis or definition in terms of absolute simples. The impression or idea of goodness, for example, will involve a complex whose "blend" of particulars has produced a wholly original complex. To ask of such a complex whether a proposed definition in terms of original simples *appears* to be exhaustively descriptive is to prejudge the case against definition. Obviously, if definition in moral enquiry is to succeed, it must be a form of definition appropriate to human sentiment, passion, feeling, etc.. So we may add to Hume's conclusion that not only are "Some of the most curious phenomena of the human mind. . .deriv'd from this property of the passions," but so also is the distinction between the methodology appropriate to moral experience and that appropriate to perception alone.

Furthermore, Hume's position here in Book II suggests that impressions and ideas are not only distinguishable in terms of "liveliness" but in more concrete terms. If ideas can combine in a mechanical manner and passions cannot, then clearly the two are basically different in kind. And if this is the case, ideas cannot be exact copies of impressions. And, indeed, this difference of kind is emphatically brought to the reader's attention in Book III. He says there,

> Now as perceptions resolve themselves into two kinds, viz. *impressions* and *ideas,* this distinction gives rise to a question, with which we shall open up our present enquiry concerning morals, *Whether 'tis by means of our* ideas *or* impressions *we distinguish betwixt vice and virtue, and pronounce an action blameable or praise-worthy?* This will immediately cut off all loose discourses

and declamations, and reduce us to something precise and exact on the present subject.[40]

Hume is not here making the point, which so much of Books II and III is concerned with, that moral distinctions are "matters of fact" and not "relations of ideas."[41] This view is in itself compatible with the position of Book I. But Hume is saying here that moral distinctions rest on impressions and not ideas. If ideas were exact copies of impressions in all respects except degree of liveliness, as Hume maintains in Book I, then moral distinctions would rest as much on ideas as on impressions, and the relevant distinction would not be between ideas and impressions, but between moral ideas and impressions, on the one hand, and non-moral ones, on the other hand.

It would be misleading to suggest, however, that Hume at any point in the *Treatise* ever directly faces the issue concerning the methodological distinctions between Book I and Books II and III. But unlike Moore who never questions the validity and applicability of part-whole analysis, Hume suggests early in Book I that the view that simples admit of no inner distinction and separation and are therefore absolute is subject to exceptions:

> Thus when a globe of white marble is presented, we receive only the impression of a white colour dispos'd in a certain form, nor are we able to separate and distinguish the colour from the form. But observing afterwards a globe of black marble and a cube of white, and comparing them with our former object, we find two separate resemblances, in what formerly seem'd, and really is, perfectly inseparable. After a little more practice of this kind, we begin to distinguish the figure from the colour by a *distinction of reason;* that is, we consider the figure and colour together, since they are in effect the same and undistinguishable; but still view them in different aspects, according to the resemblances, of which they are susceptible.[42]

Though Hume treats these "distinctions of reason" quite casually, this admittance is of great significance to moral enquiry. If simples can be distinguished in respect to their properties and qualities even though they have no separable parts, then definition of simples in a significant sense is possible. It would only be impossible on the assumption that definition in the only important sense of that word involves the reduction of a complex whole into its simplest parts. This assumption, as we have seen, lies at the heart of *Principia Ethica,* and it appears to follow from Hume's approach in Book I. Hume maintains there that these "distinctions of reason" apply only to simples, and that in the case of complex ideas part-whole analysis is applicable on the grounds that all complex ideas are composed of originally simple ideas which are ultimately separable and distinguishable. However, though this is the express view in Book I, Hume, as we saw above,[43] admits in Book II that the passions represent a major exception to this rule. Consequently, the basic assumptions of Hume's epistemology, that every idea is an exact copy of the impression which corresponds to it and that the criterion for determining the difference between ideas and impressions is one of degree of liveliness, are no longer applicable to Hume's analysis of moral phenomena.

The importance of "distinctions of reason" generally remains in the background in Books I and II where reason itself is the subject of Hume's critical attacks. In Book III, however, "distinctions of reason," plays an open and important part in moral valuation. This can be seen in a broad way by comparing Hume's treatment of representative instances where assumptions (3) and (4) above[44] fail to account for the phenomena under scrutiny. In Book I, for example, Hume is confronted with the task of finding the particular impressions which correspond to the particular ideas of space and time. In fact, the whole question of abstract ideas introduces the same question on a comprehensive level. Hume admits in the case of space and time that there are no corresponding impressions from which these ideas could be derived:

> Our internal impressions are our passions, emotions, desires and aversions: none of which, I believe, will ever be asserted to be the model, from which the idea of space is deriv'd. There remains, therefore, nothing but the senses, which can convey to us this original impression. . . But my senses convey to me only the impressions of colour'd points, dispos'd in a certain manner. If the eye is sensible of any thing farther, I desire it may be pointed out to me.[45]

But instead of reconsidering the correctness of his initial assumption that all ideas are causally dependent upon impressions, Hume seeks in Book I to circumvent the problem by begging a special category of perception. Some ideas arise not from original impressions, but from the *manner* in which impressions appear to the mind.

> The idea of time is not deriv'd from a particular impression mix'd up with the others, and plainly distinguishable from them; but arises altogether from the manner, in which impressions appear to the mind, without making one of the number. Five notes play'd on a flute give us the impression and idea of time; tho' time be not a sixth impression, which presents itself to the hearing or any other of the senses. Nor is it a sixth impression, which the mind by reflection finds in itself.[46]

> All abstract ideas are really nothing but particular ones, consider'd in a certain light. . .[47]

In Book III of the *Treatise,* Hume is confronted with a parallel problem in the area of moral perception. The problem here is to determine whether the idea of virtue has a corresponding impression. Hume's general position is that "All morality depends upon our sentiments." And this being the case, one would assume that to test the validity of a moral idea, and therefore of a moral judgment, as well, would involve the comparison of that idea or judgment with its corresponding moral impression. But Hume realizes that if this were the only criterion of validity, then morality would be purely subjective.

> A passion is an original existence, or, if you will, modification of existence, and contains not any representative quality, which ren-

61

ders it a copy of any other existence or modification. When I am angry, I am actually possest with the passion, and in that emotion have no more a reference to any other object, than when I am thirsty, or sick, or more than five foot high. 'Tis impossible, therefore, that this passion can be oppos'd by, or be contradictory to truth and reason; since this contradiction consists in the disagreement of ideas, consider'd as copies, with those objects, which they represent.[48]

If passions are "original existences" and if having a moral passion were equivalent to making a moral judgment, as Hume sometimes suggests, then disagreements over values could never be resolved.[49] And this is often the criticism leveled against Hume's position.[50] But Hume does not accept such a position as it stands. He goes on to say that valuations are expressed in the form of a judgment and that sentiment or passion alone does not therefore represent a claim: "...passions can be contrary to reason only so far as they are *accompany'd* with some judgment or opinion."[51] And secondly, although morality does depend upon our sentiments, it is only "when any action or quality of the mind pleases us *after a certain manner,* we say it is virtuous."[52] This appears to be the same sort of circumvention that we found in Book I, and indeed there is little difference between "after a certain manner" and "from the manner in which impressions appear to the mind." But Hume's moral, unlike his epistemological, theory does attempt to justify and account for the special *manner* of perception and moral experience.[53] In other words, Hume does attempt to provide an objective basis for moral judgment. And in his attempt to account for the ground of objective moral judgment, Hume not only ignores the relationship between impressions and ideas as originally formulated in Book I, but employs a basically different methodology. Ideas are no longer the exact copies of impressions, and reason, at least empirical reason, is no longer the impotent reflection of immediate experience, but plays an active part in the determination of moral decision.

One way, in fact, of reaffirming the distinction between the moral and the physical sciences is to point out their contrasting methodologies and subject matters. Book I of the *Treatise* deals with the world of human experience as a given series of simples (atomic particulars, sense-data, etc.) and knowledge as the complex of these particulars. In this respect, the human mind is viewed as the sum total of its experiences and as ultimately or theoretically resolvable into the totality of original particulars experienced. But Books II and III deal essentially with the *meaning* or *value* of the world and not merely with the givenness of our experience of it. Morality represents not merely our experience but our attitude towards that experience. The view of human knowledge and perception implicit in Book I is essentially a mechanical one; the contents of the mind are reducible to particulars *without remainder.* But the view of moral knowledge implicit in Books II and III is a fundamentally different one. Moral knowledge is there viewed, to use Dewey's words, as "the body of organized meaning by which events of the present have significance for us." The point here is that each view of knowledge presupposes not only a different content of knowledge, i.e. "organized meaning" as opposed to enumerable and describable fact, but a different methodology as well. Moore's Open Question Argument is a reflection of the content and methodology of Book I of the *Treatise*. One can isolate in one's mind the concept of a red patch (immediate perception) or of a neutron (part-whole analysis) and ask (Open Question Argument) whether or not a proposed definition exhaustively identifies the concept in a question. But if one is dealing with a concept of value, for example, that of goodness or justice, not as a particular of immediate or intuitive perception, but as "a complex or organization of meanings by which events of the present have significance for us," then there is no question of the irrelevance of Moore's negative argument. "Goodness" is neither a mental particular nor exhaustively definable. The organization of meaning is a continuing process, and moral philosophy is not so much concerned with providing exhaustive definitions of moral concepts for a given time and place as it is with defining the continuing process of organization itself. Whether Hume's answer to the latter question is an adequate one or not remains to be seen. But it is certain that if the principles and methodology underlying Hume's epistemology in Book I were accepted as representative of Hume's approach throughout the *Treatise*, then the charge against him of reducing ethics to immediate experience and therefore of committing a basic fallacy would appear to be justified.

[1]*Principia*, p. 38.

[2]*Treatise*, p. 277.

[3]*Principia*, p. 9.

[4]James Gibson, *Locke's Theory of Knowledge and Its Historical Relations*, Cambridge, Cambridge University Press, 1931, pp. 47-49.

[5]*Treatise*, p. 157.

[6]*Ibid.*, p. 157.

[7]*Ibid.*, pp. 61-62.

[8]David Hume, *Enquiry Concerning the Human Understanding*, La Salle, Illinois, Open Court Publishing Co., 1966, pp. 66-67.

[9]*Ibid.*, pp. 20-21.

[10]*Principia*, p. 8.

[11]*Treatise*, p. XX.

[12]Norman Kemp Smith, *The Philosophy of David Hume*, London, Macmillan & Co. Ltd., 1960, p. 285, *n* 1.

[13]*Treatise*, p. 13.

[14]*Ibid.*, p. 277.

[15]*Ibid.*, p. 329.

[16]*Principia*, p. 7.

[17]*Ibid.*, p. 9.

[18]*Treatise*, p. 5.

[19]*Ibid.*, p. 277.

[20]*Ibid.*, p. xxiii.

[21]*Principia*, p. 7.

[22]*Ibid.*, p. 8.

[23]*Ibid.*, p. 8.

[24]I do not wish to claim any originality for this general distinction. As far as I know, Norman Kemp Smith first suggested and defended this view in his superb work, *The Philosophy of David Hume*. But I can claim with some justification, I believe, to have supported this still largely unaccepted view in an original way, by arriving at it in an independent manner through the issue of definition. Surprisingly, Smith wholly neglects the issue of definition, which is certainly a key issue in any attempt to draw a methodological distinction in the *Treatise*. However, the most significant and interesting aspect of my own argument lies in my view that the methodological distinctions between Book I and Books II and III generate the same rigid distinction between fact and value, descriptive and evaluative judgment, reason and sentiment, that Moore's "naturalistic fallacy" claim does in respect to "all previous ethical theories, i.e. that the "naturalistic fallacy" is nothing more that the methodology of Book I of the *Treatise* applied to Books II and III.

[25]*Treatise*, p. 252.

[26]*Ibid.*, p. 252.

[27]*Ibid.*, p. 259.

[28]*Ibid.*,

[29]*Ibid.*, p. 354.

[30]*Ibid.*, p. 329.

[31]It is interesting to note that Mill ultimately acknowledges the methodological distinction in question in his *A System of Logic*. His intent is similar to Hume's in that he wishes to identify those principles and laws which pertain to all experience, and his approach is similar in that he proceeds within the mechanical framework of the composition theory: "However complex the phenomena, all their sequences and co-existences result from the laws of the separate elements. The effect produced, in social phenomena, by any complex set of circumstances amounts precisely to the sum of the effects of the circumstances taken singly... (*Philosophy of Scientific Method*, New York, Hafner Publishing, 1963, p. 332.). But though "the sum of the effects of the circumstances taken singly" account for the whole in question, Mill acknowledges the ultimate futility of this approach in dealing with social and moral phenomena: "We can never either understand in theory or command in practice the condition of a society in any one respect without taking into consideration its condition in all other respects. There is no social phenomenon which is not more or less influenced by every other part of the condition of the same society and, therefore, by every cause which is influencing any other of the contemporaneous social phenomena. (*Ibid.*, p. 335)

[32]*Treatise*, p. 2.

[33]*Ibid.*, p. 3.

[34]*Ibid.*, p. 4.

[35]*Ibid.*, p. 2.

[36]*Principia*, p. 8.

[37]*Treatise*, p. 4.

[38]*Enquiry Concerning the Human Understanding*, pp. 66-67 (Italics mine).

[39]*Treatise*, p. 366 (Italics mine).

[40]*Ibid.*, p. 456.

[41]This distinction is discussed at length in the following chapter.

[42]*Treatise*, p. 25.

[43]See above page 59.

[44]See above page 57.

[45]*Treatise*, pp. 33-34.

[46]*Ibid.*, p. 36.

[47]*Ibid.*, p. 34.

[48]*Ibid.*, p. 415.

[49]An action, or sentiment, or character is virtuous or vicious; why? because its view causes a pleasure or uneasiness of a particular kind. In giving a reason,

therefore, for the pleasure or uneasiness, we sufficiently explain the vice or virtue. To have the sense of virtue, is nothing but to *feel* a satisfaction of a particular kind from the contemplation of a character. The very *feeling* constitutes our praise or admiration. We go no farther; nor do we enquire into the cause of the satisfaction." *Treatise,* p. 471.

[50]It is interesting to note the number of people who claim that Hume believes that moral judgments are neither true nor false. The reference for this view is generally to that passage in the *Treatise* where Hume says, "'Tis impossible, therefore, they (passions, volitions, and actions) can be pronounced either true or false. . ." (page 458) But this interpretation is clearly unjustified. It is as absurd to call actions true or false as it is to call judgments themselves virtuous or vicious. The question of truth or falsity involves the relationship between judgment and sentiment, and any confusion or identification of the two leads directly to an untenable subjectivism. But though Hume often does seem to suggest such an identification, he at no point in the *Treatise* ever claims or suggests that moral judgments are neither true nor false.

[51]*Treatise,* p. 416.

[52]*Ibid.,* p. 517.

[53]In the Appendix to the *Treatise,* Hume candidly admits his failure to deal adequately with the general question of the *manner* of perception. He says there, ". . .there are two principles, which I cannot render consistent; nor is it in my power to renounce either of them, viz. *that all our distinct perceptions are distinct existences,* and *that the mind never perceives any real connexion among distinct existences.*" (p. 636) The question for ethics is whether a concept of the self as a mere bundle or series of distinct impressions will offer a satisfactory theoretical basis for moral valuation or whether a concept of the self as a unity is necessary. Ultimately Hume acknowledges the necessity of the latter alternative, though its obvious inconsistency with his epistemology remains unacknowledged and unresolved. But here it need only be pointed out that this inconsistency is not to be taken as critical of his ethical position, but only Book I and those parts of Books II and III which rely upon a concept of the self as a mere "bundle of perceptions."

CHAPTER IV

Fact and Value

Hume's epistemology in Book I of the *Treatise* rests firmly on the fundamental properties of experience. Likewise, in Books II and III, Hume contends that moral qualities refer to empirical properties, or in his terminology, "impressions." Moral judgments, therefore, ascribe moral qualities, or impressions, to human conduct, and are, as other empirical judgments, in some sense confirmable. And as also is the case with other kinds of empirical judgments, one should expect that for Hume moral judgments are inferable from other factual judgments. Yet, if the assumption were the case, Hume would quite clearly be in direct opposition to Moore's position, which rests upon the claim that any such inference involves a fallacy of a basic sort.

We have shown, I believe, that Moore's defense of the non-inferability of moral from non-moral value does not withstand philosophical scrutiny. But some would argue that Hume himself denies the validity of such inferences, so that even if Moore's understanding of such a proscription is erroneous, nevertheless, in Hume's mind such a proscription exists. This is, in fact, the very position in which we find William Frankena in his well-known criticism of Moore's position, "The Naturalistic Fallacy." Though the essay involves a detailed attempt to refute the naturalistic fallacy claim, i.e. Moore's defense of non-inferability, Frankena nevertheless maintains that "Hume's point is that ethical conclusions cannot be drawn validly from premises which are non-ethical."[1] And Ernest Gellner, who is likewise unsympathetic with Moore's position, nevertheless maintains that Moore's Naturalistic Fallacy is identical with the claim made by Hume in his often-quoted Is-Ought paragraph in the *Treatise:*

> The famous "Naturalistic Fallacy" is in essence the fallacious inference from what *is* to what *ought* to be... The *special* application of the Naturalistic Fallacy is this demonstration that key *ethical* terms cannot be defined in terms of non-ethical ones. The *general* application of it is to *any* evaluative concept... No normative issue, no question of validity, can be decided by a mere definition.[2]

But this identification of the Naturalistic Fallacy with Hume's words in the *Treatise* generates one of the most paradoxical and yet ignored questions in historical interpretation: Why, if Hume's Is-Ought paragraph is merely an expression in different words of Moore's Naturalistic Fallacy, does Hume expound a proscription which his own philosophical position so clearly violates? Could Hume, perhaps the subtlest of modern philosophers, be guilty of such an obvious inconsistency? It seems hardly possible, yet the question remains and demands an answer, for one need only recall here the enthusiastic acceptance on the part of contemporary philosophers of the claim, equally unreasonable on the surface of it, that Mill, another great naturalist, is guilty of a similar inconsistency and "fundamental fallacy."[3]

Perhaps it is something about the dogma of dichotomy itself which encourages such sweeping, yet superficial assessments of previous ethical theories. Indeed, it is on the issue of the dichotomy between fact and value that the contemporary critique of naturalism in ethics is centered. For even with the technical inadequacies of the naturalistic fallacy argument exhibited and acknowledged, the general view that there exists such a strict dichotomy remains and with it the persistent assumption that naturalistic ethical theories in some basic sense violate this separation.

However, the major difficulty facing any discussion of the fact/value dichotomy is that few moral philosophers who accept it feel obliged to defend it. If we leave aside Moore's particular defense of this view, we are left with two alternative lines of defense, though it is not at all clear what would constitute an independent defense of either one of them. One alternative is to argue that moral judgments, words, terms, concepts, expressions, etc. are different from factual judgments, words, etc. The former supposedly evaluate and express, while the latter merely describe or point to facts. In other words, an analysis of our natural languages reveals, so the argument goes, that there are within them at least two fundamentally different categories of words, concepts and judgments: evaluative and descriptive, expressions of value and assertions of fact. And not only does this show that language functions in at least two fundamentally different ways, but that there exists two logically distinct realms of *mean-*

ing and beyond, two realms of *reality*. To confuse the two different functions of language with one another, as "naturalistic ethics" supposedly does, is to commit a linguistic error which will eventually lead to unresolvable verbal disputes—hence, the view that the major task of philosophy is to perform linguistic therapy. In this respect, Moore's Naturalistic Fallacy can be interpreted as an attempt to distinguish definitively between moral and non-moral language and thereby eliminate a number of purely verbal, but "philosophically" significant, issues. And in this respect also, Moore's admission in his autobiography is worthy of note:

> I do not think that the world or the sciences would ever have suggested to me any philosophical problems. What has suggested philosophical problems to me is things which other philosophers have said about the world or sciences.[4]

But to confuse the two logically distinct realms of meaning and reality is to commit an even more damaging mistake. This involves the confusion of natural things (properties or qualities) with non-natural or moral things and consequently leads ultimately to the destruction of ethics as an autonomous realm. In short, the ultimate implication of such a confusion is a world without moral values—a one-dimensional reality. In this respect, Moore's Naturalistic Fallacy can be interpreted as the claim that "naturalistic ethical theories" destroy the autonomy of ethics:

> . . .all truths of the form "This is good in itself" are logically independent of any truth about what exists. . . All such ethical truths are true, *whatever the nature of the world may be.*[5]

The second alternative way of showing that there exists a strict dichotomy between fact and value is to argue that such a dichotomy is evidenced by the fact that no moral or value judgment (statement, proposition) can be validly inferred from premises which do not contain at least one genuinely moral premise, i.e. that value cannot be validly inferred from fact alone. A typical case of invalid moral reasoning offered by those who support this view is to give as a premise something like, "You promised to do X" and then to infer the conclusion, "You ought to do X." The argument has two prongs. The first is to argue that if one simply means in the premise the descriptive judgment that "X *is* promised by you," then the moral conclusion that "You *ought* to do X" is invalid. The movement from an "is" to an "ought" is fallacious, because we cannot have anything in the conclusion, viz. "ought", or an evaluation of any sort, which is not already contained in the premise(s). The other prong is to argue that if you mean by "You promised to do X," not only the descriptive judgment that "X is promised by you," but the evaluative judgment that "One ought to do what one has promised to do," as well, then the conclusion, "You ought to do X," can be validly drawn, but only at the cost of reaffirming the original fact/value distinction.

The major difficulty in trying to discuss and evaluate the fact/value dichotomy lies in the fact that it is not clear what is, or could be, intended as proof of it. Surely, it it could be independently shown that moral or evaluative concepts or terms are fundamentally different from factual or descriptive concepts, then it would indeed follow that moral judgments or statements containing genuinely moral concepts could not be validly inferred from purely factual judgments alone. But it does not follow conversely that even if someone could give an independent proof of the non-inferability of value from fact alone, that there exists therefore a fundamental difference between fact and value. The non-inferability of "ought" from "is" follows from the truth of the fact/value distinction, but that distinction does not follow from the truth of non-inferability. But contemporary moralists have yet to offer an independent proof of either. Most often the appeal is to some sort of *prima facie* validity of the fact/value distinction based on linguistic observations, though it is not uncommon to find the two sides of this anti-naturalist coin invoked in mutual support. Richard Hare's work, *The Language of Morals,* offers an excellent example of this circular approach combined with an appeal to linguistic distinctions.

The ethical program of *The Language of Morals* is similar to that of *Principia Ethica.* Hare makes two basic claims: 1) that ethical language in its primary usage is prescriptive and not descriptive and 2) that no imperative conclusion (primary moral concept) can be validly drawn from a set of premises which does not contain at least one imperative (primary moral concept).[6] These claims represent Moore's view that ". . .all truths of the form "This is good in itself" are logically independent of any truth about what exists."[7] And since Hare views ethics as "the logical study of the language of morals,"[8] one would expect him to provide us with a logical basis for these claims, as Moore attempts to do by his Open Question Argument. But, unfortunately, such a basis never materializes.

The first claim that ethical language in its primary usage is prescriptive and not descriptive is simply supported by an analysis of language or actual usage. A prescriptive moral judgment is one which answers the question "What shall I do?," while a descriptive judgment answers the question "What is the nature of such and such?" Since an answer to the former question would be in the imperative mood, for example, "You ought to. . . ," no moral judgment can be construed to be a pure statement of fact. All moral judgments contain imperatives and as such are *sui generis.*

But it is not at all clear what constitutes the fundamental basis of this argument. Hare seems to imply that the distinction between evaluative and descriptive statements is *prima facie* recognizable in at least the majority of cases in ordinary discourse. But it is clearly not *prima facie* the case that "X ought to do so and so," for example, involves a non-factual prescription. It may in fact be wholly reducible to the set of conditions under which X could actualize so and so. The suggestion has been offered that we call these conditions "institutional" ones, so that within certain institutions, certain typically evaluative terms such as "ought" receive their factual basis.[9] In other words, all institutionalized forms of moral evaluation are at the same time factual. Moral values are, in short, institutional facts.

However, I do not see why we need to resort to this sort of explanation.

It is obvious that such an answer is merely definitional until one can answer the more basic question concerning the moral basis of our institutions themselves. Interestingly, Hare rejects Searle's "institutional" defense of factual basis of morality on precisely these grounds, that "institutions" cannot and do not account for the force or the "oughtness" of moral obligation.[10] If our institutions were the ultimate ground of obligation then surely we could, as Hare points out, simply define our obligations. After all, one of the basic functions of moral reasoning is, in the first place, to distinguish between those institutions or activities of institutions which are compatible with our moral values and those which are not. If we could defend the "oughtness" of keeping one's promises by appealing to the so-called institution of promising or promise-keeping, then equally we could defend the American involvement in Vietnam by appealing to the institution of war or war-making.

But rather than go a step further as Hume does and exhibit the "naturalistic" ground of institutions themselves, i.e. the ground of institutions within the natural and social experience of man, Hare opts for a self-justifying concept of obligation, on the basis that any such "naturalistic" identification of value would involve a basic fallacy. How can we, then, identify what Hare means by calling moral judgments prescriptive? In other words, what makes an "imperative" or "prescription" distinctively moral? Hare's answer is that assenting to a descriptive statement involves believing, whereas assenting to a prescriptive statement involves doing something.[11] But this distinction is hardly decisive. This move simply transfers the problem: Why shouldn't a description involve "doing something," as well as simply "believing something"? In very elementary cases "believing" and "doing" can be distinguished, though I am not sure that the distinction serves any valuable purpose in these cases. For example, between "Jones has red hair" and "Jones ought to pay me," the distinction between believing and doing is clear, but between the interesting cases of "Jones promised to pay me" and "Jones ought to pay me," the distinction in itself is far from decisive.

But Hare himself admits that this distinction over-simplifies the matter and refers us to a later section of the argument. When we turn to the later section of the book, we find that Hare attempts to support the general claim that evaluative and descriptive statements are fundamentally different on the basis of the following scheme:

(1) 'X is required in order to conform to the standard which people generally accept (statement of sociological fact);

(2) 'I have a feeling that I ought to do X' (statement of psychological fact);

(3) 'I ought to do X' (value judgment).[12]

Hare's problem is to explain why (3) is not reducible to (1) or (2), i.e. why an evaluation is not reducible to a form of description. Hare's answer is curiously weak. He proposes "to get over this difficulty in the only way, by making it a matter of definition."[13] He says,

I propose to say that the test, whether someone is using the judgment 'I ought to do X' as a value-judgment or not is, 'Does he or does he not recognize that if he assents to the judgment, he must also assent to the command "Let me do X"?'[14]

However, this definition does not provide a solution to the problem. We are still left with no *substantial* way to distinguish between descriptive and evaluative judgments. Since Hare seeks to avoid all questions of moral psychology,[15] we must ultimately take the word of the agent. And we generally assume that when someone says "I promise to repay this loan," he means as well "I ought to repay this loan." In other words, Hare fails to deal with basis or ground of moral distinctions, but deals only with the verbal distinctions which can sometimes be drawn. But Hare does not appear to be greatly disturbed by this result, for his admission is directly to the point:

> Thus I am not here claiming to prove anything substantial about the way in which we use language; I am merely suggesting a terminology which, if applied to the study of moral language, will I am satisfied, prove illuminating.[16]

What started out as a *prima facie* distinction between moral terms or concepts in their primary sense and factual terms and concepts, has ended up as a terminological definition, which is subject neither to confirmation nor disconfirmation. This can hardly satisfy the major need of distinguishing morality in its primary sense or usage from all other areas of discourse and experience. However, Hare goes on to claim that "I ought to do X" is "intractably evaluative" and that this "is due ultimately to the impossibility mentioned earlier of deriving imperatives from indicatives."[17] Thus we have returned full-swing to the basic assumption that no "ought-proposition" can be inferred from an "is-proposition," an assumption which Hare originally supports with the claim that there exists a fundamental dichotomy between prescriptive and descriptive judgments, but which he now uses to support that claim.

But, as was mentioned above, even if it could be proven that no "ought-proposition" can be validly inferred from an "is-proposition," it would not prove that there exists a fundamental dichotomy between fact and value. It is the non-inferability of "ought" from "is" that rests upon the assumption that there exists a dichotomy between fact and value. In order to avoid the circularity of Hare's position, one must give first of all an independent proof of the fact/value distinction, exhibiting its nature and areas of applicability. Indeed, if this attempt were made, it might well turn out that the fact/value distinction is not applicable to the area of morality, not because we can never distinguish fact from vlaue, but because moral language might prove to be a unity of fact and value, description and evaluation, of such a manner that within genuine moral experience the two are ultimately inseparable.

In this respect, the related question whether ethics can be reduced wholly to statements of fact may be very misleading. It is commonly assumed that the question of the reducibility of value to fact depends upon the question of inferability, i.e. that it is only through definition or some such other *deductive* model that we can, if at all, reduce value to fact. But it may be the case that moral concepts and/or judgments (statements, claims, etc.) are neither wholly factual nor wholly evaluative in any instances of moral discourse, simple or complex. It may be the case, in other words, that moral language is both descriptive and evaluative, not in the sense, however, of two related but distinct functions combined in one act, viz. a moral judgment, but in the sense of being itself distinguishable from all other types of judgment. The object of analysis, then, would be to provide a criterion for identifying genuine moral judgment and not for distinguishing between two supposedly separate and separable functions within that judgment. Moral language, to rephrase Hare, may prove to be intractably moral; in which case, only philosophical analysis, as opposed to analysis which is merely linguistic, can hope to exhibit its peculiarly moral nature. Linguistic analysis, or whatever we wish to call an approach does not go beyond the analysis of ordinary discourse, must accept as genuinely moral all verbal expressions containing what are considered to be genuine moral terms, e.g. "ought." It is for this reason that Hare is forced to conclude that "I ought to do X" is "intractably evaluative."[18] But once we accept a verbal or linguistic criterion of moral judgment, we are not only forced by our reasoning to draw a distinction between supposedly descriptive and evaluative terms, but must resort in the final analysis, like Hare, to definition in order to defend that distinction.[19]

It is interesting to note also that Hare fails to recognize any substantial distinction between his approach to moral enquiry and Hume's, for he refers the reader, by way of support for his own position, to "Hume's celebrated observation on the impossibility of deducing an 'ought'-proposition from a series of 'is'-propositions."[20] It is important, then, that we consider Hume's position on the question of the inferability of "ought" from "is," not only in respect to his general position, but in respect to the common view that Hume supports a strict dichotomy between fact and value.

The evidence which is offered by those who like Hare contend that Hume denies the inferability of "ought" from "is" and thereby acknowledges a strict dichotomy between fact and value is compacted in one paragraph. That paragraph is the last one in the section of the *Treatise* entitled "Moral Distinctions not derived from Reason." I quote it in full and hereafter for the sake of convenience I shall refer to it simply as the Is-Ought paragraph.

I cannot forbear adding to these reasonings an observation which may, perhaps, be found of some importance. In every system of morality, which I have hitherto met with, I have always remark'd, that the author proceeds for some time in the ordinary way of reasoning, and establishes the being of a God, or makes osbervations concerning human affairs; when of a sudden I am surpris'd to find, that instead of the usual copulation of propositions, *is*, and *is not*, I meet with no proposition that is not connected with an *ought* or an *ought not*. This change is imperceptible; but is, however, of the last consequence. For as this *ought*, or *ought not*, expresses some new relation or affirmation, 'tis necessary that it should be observ'd and explain'd; and at the same time that a reason should be

73

given, for what seems altogether inconceivable, how this new relation can be a deduction from others, which are entirely different from it. But as authors do not commonly use this precaution, I shall presume to recommend it to the readers; and am persuaded, that this small attention wou'd subvert all the vulgar systems of morality, and let us see, that the distinction of vice and virtue is not founded merely on the relations of objects, nor is perceiv'd by reason.[21]

The Is-Ought paragraph appears to contain three major elements:

a) Previous systems of morality proceed in the "ordinary way," first establishing the being of a God or making observations concerning human affairs expressed in propositions with the copulation "is" or "is not."

b) These same systems then proceed to introduce "imperceptively" propositions connected with an "ought" or "ought not." As "ought" and "ought not" are entirely different from "is" and "is not" and express some new relation or affirmation, it is necessary to explain and defend this step.

c) Paying attention to this step will subvert all vulgar systems of morality and let us see that moral distinctions are founded not merely on the relations of objects, nor are perceived by reason.

Hume is not denying that value judgments are expressed with an "is." Most often they are, especially in Hume's own writings. Moreover, the section which the Is-Ought paragraph concludes is intended to show that moral distinctions are impressions and impressions are matters of fact, according to Hume. But a) should not be taken to imply either that all moral distinctions are expressed by "is" (or "is not") or that all moral distinctions can be thus accounted for. The question whether or not "ought" and "ought not" are acceptable moral distinctions and, if they are, in what sense, cannot be answered on the basis of the Is-Ought paragraph alone.

However, b) clearly says that "ought" and "ought not" are distinct from "is" and "is not" and the introduction of the former into our moral systems must be defended and explained. But we cannot on this basis alone conclude that Hume draws a logical distinction between "ought" and "is." To assume this would be tantamount to assuming that at this point in the *Treatise* Hume draws a distinction which undermines the program of the rest of Book II and the whole of Book III. And if we interpret Moore's Naturalistic Fallacy in terms of a rigid distinction between fact and value, it would be tantamount to assuming, as Hare does, that Hume is here cautioning against a common fallacy which he then goes on to commit himself.

There is, of course, another alternative. One could argue both that Hume supports the view that there exists a logical distinction between "is" and "ought" and yet, at the same time, does not commit the Naturalistic Fallacy, by arguing that Hume denies the validity of "ought" as a moral category. If Hume rejects "ought" as valid moral category, then surely he cannot be guilty of reducing "ought" to "is" or inferring one from the other. This, in essence, is the alternative that Norman Kemp Smith takes. He says in his *The Philosophy of David Hume*, "In other words, there is, on Hume's theory of morals, no such thing as *moral* obligation, in the strict sense of the term."[22] Professor Smith's reasoning is that since Hume does not, and can not within his theory, develop an intrinsically self-justifying concept of virtue and obligation, Hume cannot validly draw a distinction between "is" and "ought." But this alternative is unacceptable for a number of reasons, though it should be sufficient to recognize the fact that Hume defines moral obligation in terms of virtuous acts. Thus, not only is Hume's treatment of obligation co-extensive with his treatment of virtue, but it is only by rejecting or qualifying his position in respect to the latter, that we can question the former.

However, all we can conclude at this point is that to Hume "ought" and "is" are distinct moral categories, that one cannot be deduced from the other, and that "ought" and "ought not" must be accounted for. It does not follow that because "ought" and "is" are distinct and that "ought" is not deducible from "is" that the two therefore have distinct logical grounds. It may be the case that "ought" has a factual, naturalistic ground, just as does "is." Otherwise, one would have to assume that because two properties have a non-deductive relationship they therefore imply distinct logical grounds. "Ought" and "is" may both have factual, naturalistic grounds, yet not be reducible one to the other.

But if "ought" is not deducible from "is", and equally does not carry any *prima facie* validity, how then can we account for it? This question, in fact, introduces the task of Books II and III of the *Treatise*. Moral obligation, like all other moral distinctions, is grounded in approval and disapproval, according to Hume. Consequently, the major task of Hume's moral system is to account for the general mechanism of approval and disapproval, that is, to develop first of all a general theory of valuation, and then to develop within it the specific criteria for *moral* valuation. "Ought," as Hume says in the Is-Ought paragraph, implies a new "affirmation." Unlike "is," "ought" not only serves to describe the factual conditions of a moral situation, but also to express the peculiarly moral quality of it. "Is" may serve to express our personal, subjective feelings of approval and disapproval, but can never serve to express our *moral* feelings. It is for this reason that we introduce into our moral systems peculiarly moral terms such as "ought" and "ought not." As Hume expresses it in the *Enquiry*,

> The distinction, therefore, between these species of sentiment being so great and evident, language must soon be moulded upon it, and must invent a peculiar set of terms, in order to express those universal sentiments of censure or approbation, which arise from humanity, or from views of general usefulness and its contrary.[23]

To account for this "peculiar set of terms," viz. moral predicates, in other words, to exhibit the ground of that approval and disapproval we distinguish as *moral,* constitutes the fundamental task of moral enquiry.

But nowhere in the *Treatise,* much less in the Is-Ought paragraph, does Hume say that "ought" lacks a factual basis. "Ought," like "virtuous," "good," "praiseworthy," etc., finds its source in the general mechanism of approval and disapproval, and it is only within this broad framework that we can seek to determine what Hume holds to be the relationship between "is" and "ought," and the relationship of both to morality.

It is Hume's position in respect to c) which clears the ground for the "naturalistic" approach to morality in Books II and III. In c), Hume tells us that if we note the change from a) to b), we will accomplish two things: 1) we will subvert all the "vulgar" systems of morality, and 2) prove that the distinction of vice and virtue is not founded merely on the relations of objects, nor is perceived by reason. The basis for these claims rests on one of the fundamental assumptions of Hume's philosophical position, namely, that there is no philosophical justification for believing that objects exist independently of human perception. The "vulgar" believe that we have immediate perception of independently and continuously existing objects:

> ...the vulgar confound perceptions and objects, and attribute a distinct continu'd existence to the very things they feel and see.[24]

Since moral properties are impressions, they are in this respect similar to objects of immediate perception:

> Vice and virtue may be compar'd to sounds, colours, heat and cold, which, according to modern philosophy, are not qualities in objects, but perceptions in the mind.[25]

The vulgar are led to assume, therefore, that since moral impressions, like objects of immediate perception, appear to be objective qualities of objects existing independently, moral qualities exist independently of human perception. Assuming this, the vulgar identify their perceptions with vice and virtue, what one ought and ought not to do. That is, the vulgar assume that their perceptions are in themselves sufficient to account for vice and virtue and to justify moral obligation. For, if moral perception were in fact a face-to-face apprehension of vice and virtue, something along the lines of Moore's view of "intuition" or "reflective judgment," then surely our judgment of right and wrong would be infallible and, as such, carry its own justification:

> For since all actions and sensations of the mind are known to us by consciousness, they must necessarily appear in every particular what they are, and be what they appear. Every thing that enters the mind, being in *reality* as the perception, 'tis impossible any thing shou'd to *feeling* appear different. This were to suppose, that even where we are most intimately conscious, we might be mistaken.[26]

But though immediate perception leads us to *feel* unmistaken about the objective content of consciousness, we are often, however, mistaken. And it is the very gap between immediate perception and *real existence* that Hume refers to when he speaks of the distinction between "is" and "ought." It is the search for some reasonable standard of objective moral judgment that engages Hume in Books II and III of the *Treatise* and which results in the subversion of all vulgar systems of morality.

The final claim of the Is-Ought paragraph that vice and virtue are not perceived by reason is somewhat more involved and a full discussion of it would carry us away from our intended goal.[27] But a brief comment on one aspect of this claim is appropriate. Hume's criticism here refers to those moral theories which attempt to identify morality with rational conduct. Prior to the Is-Ought paragraph, Hume observes that,

> Nothing is more usual in philosophy, and even in common life, than to talk of the combat of passion and reason, to give the preference to reason, and assert that men are only so far virtuous as they conform themselves to its dictates.[28]

The identification of vice and virtue with rational conduct would obviously eliminate the Is-Ought problem, for a deduction from what *is* the case to what *ought* to be the case would involve a demonstrable rational process. In short, on this view, one ought to do what is rationally implied by the circumstances.

Hume has two objections against this view. The first is that the moral relations that reason can supposedly discover can never be specified so as to be intelligible or to exclude absurd cases such as animals or inanimate objects. The second is that these relations are not obligatory; that is to say, "no relation can ever alone produce any action."[29] Thus Hume observes,

> Animals are susceptible of the same relations, with respect to each other, as the human species, and therefore wou'd also be susceptible of the same morality, if the essence of morality consisted in these relations. Their want of a sufficient degree of reason may hinder them from perceiving the duties and obligations of morality, but can never hinder these duties from existing; since they must antecedently exist, in order to their being perceiv'd. Reason must find them, and can never produce them. This argument deserves to be weigh'd as being, in my opinion, entirely decisive.[30]

These acts which we find in the animal world bear no relational characteristics different from those of the human world. Reason, therefore, cannot draw the distinction between morally indifferent and morally significant events or facts. Moreover, the same argument is sufficient to show that such *a priori* relations, even if intelligible, would not move the will:

> 'Tis a will or choice that determines a man to kill his parent: and they are the laws of matter and motion that determine a sapling to destroy the oak from which it sprung. Here then the same relations have different causes; but still the relations are the same: And as their discovery is not in both cases attended with the notion of immorality, it follows, that that notion does not arise from such a discovery.[31]

Applicability to non-human objects is a decisive argument against the view that moral distinctions are relations discoverable by reason. The same argument, therefore, further undermines the "vulgar" view that moral distinctions or properties exist independently of human perception. As long as moral distinctions are regarded as relations existing independently of human perception, morality will apply equally to animals and inanimate objects. To say, then, that someone *ought* to do something is not to say *merely* that something is the case; there is nothing, either *a priori* or otherwise, about an object, event, or circumstance, discoverable by the understanding, which *alone* would oblige us to act in a certain manner.

By concluding the Is-Ought paragraph with the qualification that ". . . the distinction of vice and virtue is not founded merely on the relations of objects," Hume points to the distinguishing characteristic of "naturalistic ethics," namely, to the view that moral valuation involves the unity of our faculties of perception, of thought and feeling. In Book III Hume writes,

> Philosophy is commonly divided into *speculative* and *practical;* and as morality is always comprehended under the latter division, it is supposed to influence our passions and actions, and to go beyond the calm and indolent judgements of the understanding.[32]

No amount of knowledge of fact, no amount of reasoning alone, can ever move the will or oblige us to do what we are in fact obliged to do. Moral distinctions must be such as to influence action and if "reason (understanding, knowledge) alone can never be the motive to any action of the will,"[33] then sentiment (passion, feeling) must also contribute to the source of moral distinctions. And this conclusion is even more emphatic in the case of obligation than in moral valuation in general, since in the case of obligation we do not simply *feel* towards an object, but are moved to *act* on it. Consequently, in respect to the supposed dichotomy between fact and value, the fundamental question confronting Hume in his moral enquiry is not whether "ought" can be inferred from "is," but concerns the manner in which reason and sentiment combine to produce genuine moral valuation. Once it is acknowledged that reason alone can never determine vice and virtue, the issue of the inferability of "ought" from "is" is no longer relevant. Fact and value are obviously related in all moral valuation, but it is not by finding the correct deductive model, but rather by developing a comprehensive, "naturalistic" framework of valuation in general that we can hope to exhibit their relationship.

The conclusion of the Is-Ought paragraph carries us to a point in the *Treatise* where the positive task of Hume's general argument begins. So far Hume has argued *against* the view that moral distinctions are perceived by reason, that "ought" can be deduced from "is," and the vulgar view that morality is simply a matter of observable and describable fact, that what *ought* to be is identical with what *is*. But if sentiment plays a fundamental role in all moral valuation, how then do we distinguish moral sentiment from sentiment in general? More specifically, since all sentiment moves us, how do we decide which movement is in fact a movement to our duty and which is not? Or, in general terms, how do we distinguish moral valuation from valuation in general, good character from good music? Hume must provide us, in other words, with a criterion for identifying moral sentiment, in particular, and moral valuation, in general. If such a task is successful, we will then be in a position to answer the broad question concerning the program of Hume's moral theory and to a significant extent of naturalistic ethics.

[1]William Frankena, "The Naturalistic Fallacy," reprinted in W. Sellars and J. Hospers, *Readings in Ethical Theory*. New York, Appleton-Century-Crofts, Inc., 1952, pp. 104-05.

[2]Ernest Gellner, *Words and Things*, Boston, Beacon Press, 1959, p. 37.

[3]I am familiar with two excellent defenses of Mill against the charge of fundamental inconsistency: Everett Hall's "The 'Proof' of Utility in Bentham and Mill," (see above p. 2.) and Berel Lang and Gary Stahl, "Mill's 'Howlers' and the Logic of Naturalism," *Philosophy and Phenomenological Research*, June, 1969.

[4]G.E. Moore, "An Autobiography," in *The Philosophy of G.E. Moore*, ed. by Paul Arthur Schilpp, New York, Tudor Publishing Company, 1952, p. 14.

[5]G.E. Moore, *International Journal of Ethics*, Oct. 1903, p. 116.

[6]Richard Hare, *The Language of Morals*, Oxford, Clarendon Press, 1952, p. 28.

[7]See above, pp. 12ff.

[8]*The Language of Morals*, p. v.

[9]John Searle, "How to Derive 'Ought' from 'Is'," *Philosophical Review*, Vol. 73 (1964), pp. 43-58.

[10]Richard Hare, "The Promising Game," *Revue Internationale de Philosophie*, No. 70 (1964), pp. 398-412.

[11]Richard Hare, *The Language of Morals*, Oxford, Clarendon Press, 1952, p. 20.

[12]*Ibid.*, p. 167.

[13]*Ibid.*, p. 168.

[14]*Ibid.*, p. 168-69.

[15]*Ibid.*, p. 169.

[16]*Ibid.*, p. 169.

[17]*Ibid.*, p. 171.

[18]See above, p.

[19]*Ibid.*, p.

[20]*The Language of Morals*, p. 29.

[21]*Treatise*, pp. 469-70.

[22]Norman Kemp Smith, *The Philosophy of David Hume*, Macmillan & Company, London, 1960, p. 200-02.

[23]*Enquiry*, p. 274.

[24]*Treatise*, p. 193.

[25]*Ibid.*, p. 469.

[26]*Ibid.*, p. 190.

[27]See Rachael Kydd's *Reason and Conduct in Hume's Moral Theory* for an excellent and thorough discussion of this point.

[28]*Treatise*, p. 413.
[29]*Ibid.*, p. 466.
[30]*Ibid.*, p. 468.
[31]*Ibid.*, p. 467.
[32]*Ibid.*, p. 457.
[33]

CHAPTER V

Against the view that ethical theory is an independent, theoretical enterprise with no direct relationship to conduct and ultimately concerned only with "What *things* have intrinsic value, and in what degrees?"[1] Hume views ethical theory as an attempt to exhibit and explain those factors and principles underlying and justifying our value judgments. Where Moore sees the basic task of ethical theory in terms of finding the one correct verbal description or definition of goodness,[2] since he believes that it is by means of such definitions that ethical theorists provide answers to the question "What *things* have intrinsic value?," Hume is concerned to answer the more basic question concerning the *ground* or basis of morality. We do make moral distinctions. This is a fact of experience. All these instances of human beings making moral distinctions are, for Hume, "moral facts" relevant to the task of explaining those distinctions in terms of the most general reasons or principles discoverable. Book II of the *Treatise* is an attempt to identify and analyze these "moral facts," the natural sentiments and constitution of human nature, and Book III is an attempt to explain those "facts" in terms of general principles. This is the broad program for moral philosophy recommended by Hume.

Both Hume and Moore wish to provide an analysis or definition of goodness, as well as our other basic moral concepts. The crucial issue between them, however, is whether we should seek our definitions of moral concepts in terms of reason and reflective judgment, on the one hand, or in terms of human sentiment, custom, and practical need, on the other. If we agree with Moore that our reflective judgment or intuition is the sole and proper source of moral wisdom, then we ought to look to it for a definition of goodness. But if we agree with Hume that "Justice is certainly approv'd of for no other reason, than because it has a tendency to the public good. . ."[3] and that "Morality. . .is more properly felt than judg'd of,"[4] then we ought to look to human sentiment and interest for our definitions and principles.

Hume often suggests, however, that morality is concerned exclusively with sentiment and that reason or judgment as such plays no primary role in moral affairs. He is especially suggestive of this position at those points in his argument where he is concerned to exhibit both primacy of passion and the impotence of reason in human conduct. His well-known statement in Book II that "Reason is, and ought only to be, the slave of the passions"[5] and his equally forceful reaffirmation of this view at the beginning of Book III that "reason is perfectly inert"[6] seem to leave no place in morality for reason, practical or otherwise. But this position not only contradicts his later view that understanding, as well as sentiment, is requisite in all our actions,[7] but is clearly inadequate to provide a general standard of morality or account for those specifically social virtues, such as justice, which depend in large part on a rational understanding of social relations.

The question concerning the relationship between reason and sentiment in Hume's ethical theory is a difficult one, for Hume himself seems never to have come to a definite conclusion. Perhaps in fact a definite conclusion concerning this relationship is not a real possibility, not so much because of the difficulty of the question, as of the nature of reason and sentiment themselves in human conduct. The question, in other words, may be a relative, and not an absolute, one depending more on specific circumstances and character than on the general nature and role of judgment and reason. This view seems to be supported by Hume on more than one occasion. He says in Book II while discussing the influences of the will,

> The common error of metaphysicians has lain in ascribing the direction of the will entirely to one of these principles, and supposing the other to have no influence. Men often act knowingly against their interest; for which reason, the view of the greatest possible good does not always influence them. Men often counteract a violent passion in prosecution of their own interests and designs; it is not, therefore, the present uneasiness alone which determines them. In general we may observe that both these principles operate on the will; and where they are contrary, that either of them prevails, according to the *general* character or *present* disposition of the person.[8]

But though we cannot find a specific conclusion on this question in Hume's writings, yet he does, I believe, offer us the general outlines of a solution. We saw that in the Is-Ought paragraph Hume rejects the efficacy of reason in perceiving or determining moral distinctions. Yet we remarked also that he qualifies this rejection by adding that reason *alone* could never draw such distinctions: "...the distinction of vice and virtue is not founded *merely* on the relations of objects."[9] He likewise qualifies his criticism of reason in Book II where he says,

> ...the course of the argument leads us to conclude, that since vice and virtue are not discoverable merely by reason, or the comparison of ideas, it must be by means of some impression or sentiment they occasion, that we are able to mark the difference betwixt them. Our decisions concerning moral rectitude and depravity are evidently perceptions; and as all perceptions are either impressions or ideas, the exclusion of the one is a convincing argument for the other. Morality, therefore, is more properly felt than judged of;.. [10]

By "properly" Hume does not mean "exclusively," but merely that sentiment and not reason is the more basic of the two. This suggests, therefore, that the ultimate question of moral enquiry is not to decide between reason and sentiment, but to determine the manner of their relationship in moral valuation. Moreover, in his definition of moral obligation Hume emphatically qualifies the view that sentiment alone is the sole ground of moral distinctions:

> All morality depends upon our sentiments; and when any action or quality of the mind pleases us *after a certain manner,* we say it is virtuous; and when the neglect or non-performance of it displeases us *after a like manner,* we say that we lie under an obligation to perform it.[11]

If this statement were taken literally, that is without any qualification or explanation of "after a certain manner," then Hume would indeed be saying that the possession of a sentiment is equivalent to making a moral judgment. "I believe X to be virtuous" is equivalent on this reading to "X pleases me." And this view follows strictly from Hume's concept of "passion" in Book II coupled with the unqualified premise that all morality depends upon sentiment. A passion is defined by Hume in Book II as

> ...an original existence, or, if you will, modification of existence, and contains not any representative quality, which renders it a copy of any other existence or modification. When I am angry, I am actually possest with the passion, and in that emotion have no more a reference to any other object, than when I am thirsty, or sick, or more than five foot high.[12]

Thus, if a passion is complete in itself and has no reference to any other object and if all morality depends upon sentiment (passion), then morality can extend no farther than the subjective conditions of immediate experience. And, indeed,

> Vice and virtue, therefore, may be compar'd to sounds, colours, heat and cold, which, according to modern philosophy, are not qualities in objects, but perceptions in the mind.[13]

C. D. Broad's treatment of Hume's moral position is just one instance where Hume's words are taken literally. Broad reduces Hume's position to one of pure subjective description supported by a social head-count. Broad recognizes the fact that Hume seeks to be objective as well as provide some basis for valid moral debate, so he concedes that "X is good" must mean something more than "I approve of X here and now." But since, according to Broad's understanding of Hume, "I approve of X here and now" is as far as individual moral judgment extends, "X is good" must represent, if correct, that most people do, or have, or would, approve of X. Broad says in his *Five Types of Ethical Theory,*

> Hume's theory is that "*x* is good" means that the contemplation of *x* will call forth an emotion of approval in all or most men on all or most occasions. Such statements as this can be argued about and supported or refuted by observation and collection of statistics.[14]

And at a later point he draws the implications of such a position:

> . . .the logical consequence of Hume's theory is not that in disputes on moral questions there comes a point beyond which we can only say *"de gustibus non est disputandum"*. The logical consequence of his theory is that all such disputes *could* be settled, and that the way to settle them is to collect statistics of how people do in fact feel. And to me this kind of answer seems utterly irrelevant to this kind of question. If I am right in this, Hume's theory must be false.[15]

But that this is only a partial and therefore mistaken view of Hume's position is suggested in the first place by Hume's insistence that moral valuation involves a special "manner" of perception: "when any action or quality of the mind pleases us *after a certain manner,* we say it is virtuous." These are Hume's italics. He is emphasizing in fact the fundamental task facing him and any other ethical theorist who seeks to formulate and defend a standard of moral valuation. It is not, however, unreasonable that Hume's call for an objective standard has been poorly received by so many critics and reduced to what is ultimately a subjective standpoint, for his ultimate position is in many significant ways incompatible with his early pronouncements on the role of reason in human conduct and the relationship between reflection and immediate perception.[16] But just as the emphasis on the view that ideas are exact copies of impressions in Book I changes to a concern with the distinction between reason and passion, or relations of ideas and matters of fact in Book II, so also does Hume's view of the general impotency of reason and the primacy of human sentiment in human conduct become modified as the problem of a general moral standard arises in Book III. The most effective and natural way to exhibit these modifications is by considering how Hume does in fact analyze representative moral concepts.

The question of moral approval and disapproval (approbation and disapprobation, right and wrong, vice and virtue) is, of course, only a part of the question of valuation in general. "Good" is predicable of health and cooking, for example, as well as morally approved conduct. It must be admitted, however, that Hume often makes it difficult for the reader to draw this distinction, especially in Book II where "passion" or "sentiment" is employed to cover all the propensities and non-intellectual "springs of action" in man. One is led to believe in this respect that Hume's moral theory is merely an extension of his general theory of practical action. In fact Hume comes very close at times to drawing such a connection. He compares the moral sentiments to those other "perceptions of the mind" which are products of sensation in general:

> [Moral sentiment] is a matter of fact, but 'tis the object of feeling, not of reason. It lies in yourself, not in the object. So that when you pronounce any action or character to be vicious, you mean nothing, but that from the constitution of your nature you have a feeling or sentiment of blame from the contemplation of it. Vice and virtue, therefore, may be compar'd to sounds, colours, heat and cold, which. . .are not qualities in objects, but perceptions in the mind.[17]

But in the final analysis Hume does draw the distinction between moral and non-moral sentiments and recognizes the fundamental importance of the question of the validity or verification of these sentiments.

> 'Tis evident, that under the term *pleasure,* we comprehend sensations, which are very different from each other, and which have only such a distant resemblance, as is requisite to make them be express'd by the same abstract term. A good composition of music and a bottle of good wine equally produce pleasure; and what is more, their goodness is determin'd merely by the pleasure. But shall we say upon that account, that the wine is harmonious, or the music of a good flavour?[18]

And he says elsewhere,

> Our servant, if diligent and faithful, may excite stronger sentiments of love and kindness than Marcus Brutus, as represented in history; but we say not, upon that account, that the former character is more laudable than the latter.[19]

How then do we distinguish moral pleasure from other sorts of pleasure? Hume offers one basic criterion:

> Nor is every sentiment of pleasure and pain. . .of that *peculiar* kind which makes us praise or condemn. . . It is only when a character is considered in general, without reference to our particular interest, that it causes such a feeling or sentiment as denominates it morally good or evil.[20]

Without such an impartial consideration of the qualities of an agent's character, resolution of our moral disputes would be impossible.

> . . .every particular person's pleasure and interest being different, it is impossible men could ever agree in their sentiments and judgements, unless they chose some common point of view, from which they might survey their object, and which might cause it to appear the same to all of them. Now, in judging of characters, the only interest or pleasure which appears the same to every spectator, is

that of the person himself whose character is examined, or that of persons who have a connection with him. And, though such interests and pleasures touch us more faintly than our own, yet, being more constant and universal, they counterbalance the latter even in practice, and are alone admitted in speculation as the standard of virtue and morality. They alone produce that particular feeling or sentiment on which moral distinctions depend.[21]

Hume is saying here that an agent's character or a quality of his character must be considered for what it is and apart from any reference to our own particular interest or to the interests of those near to us. In order then to approve or disapprove morally of a quality or character, I must eliminate from my contemplation of it any relations it might bear to my personal interests and any influences which are contingent upon my standpoint in time and space. I approve of many things which I would disapprove of from a narrower or selfish point of view. To cite Hume's own example, from an impartial point of view we may approve of the qualities of our enemies, though they prove harmful to us.[22] It cannot be the case, therefore, that the common interpretation of Hume to the effect that "X is good" means "I approve of X" is a correct one. On the basis of Hume's analysis, one may genuinely approve of an object and yet that object may not be good. For "X is good" means, according to Hume, "I approve of X and my approval of X has resulted from an impartial contemplation of X." That is to say, I have contemplated X as it is in itself and apart from any relation it might have to my particular interests. Now, it may be the case that I am mistaken in my moral evaluation of X. I may have a completely mistaken idea of the true nature of X or may not have succeeded in eliminating from my contemplation of it any particular relation it might bear to me. In which case, my approval is not *moral* approval, and X may or may not be *morally* good. A more thorough understanding of whatever object I am attempting to judge morally and a more thoroughly abstract contemplation of it could (and is very likely to) result in a change in my attitude and feeling toward it. And for the same reasons, an action, character, or quality may be moral and at the same time disapproved of by the majority. Hume's argument in no way leads to the identification of consensus opinion with moral right and wrong. Indeed, just as one individual of a group or even of a whole society may alone exhibit a moral character or who alone may follow a moral course of action in a given circumstance (as Plato says of Socrates), so also may one individual alone in a given society make a proper moral judgment. Hume does say repeatedly in both the *Treatise* and the *Enquiry* that custom and experience together constitute the great guide of human life, but he says this more in reference to the need in moral philosophy to recognize and accommodate the *de facto* constitution and interests of man than to an acceptance of custom and experience as moral standards. Obviously, if "ought" is to imply "can," which it must if morality is to have a practical effect on human behavior, then the factual conditions of human behavior must be compatible with our moral maxims. You cannot make it a moral maxim that one love his neighbor in a world where hating one's neighbor is often a condition of survival. "Ought" and "is," moral judgment and custom, are intimately related and inter-dependent, according to Hume, but a strict identification of the two can only lead to confusions and obvious absurdities. Hume makes this quite clear in the *Treatise* before beginning his moral enquiry:

> Consider well the consequences of such a principle [the strict acceptance of custom]. By this means you cut off entirely all science and philosophy: You proceed upon one singular quality of the imagination, and by a parity of reasoning must embrace all of them: And you expressly contradict yourself: since this maxim must be built on the preceding reasoning, which will be allow'd to be sufficiently refin'd and metaphysical.[23]

Two fundamental points follow from Hume's analysis of moral valuation. The first is that since moral approval does not rest merely upon sentiment, we can resolve—to a point—our moral disagreements. This is to say, that to a point we can develop objective moral standards. The second point is that reason plays a necessary role in moral valuation. Reason is not merely the "slave of the passions," but is as necessary to moral sentiment as sentiment is to action itself. It was pointed out above that according to C. D. Broad Hume does not provide us with a sufficient basis for the resolution of our moral disputes; we can only say *de gustibus non est disputandum.* Broad interprets "X is good" to mean something more than "I approve of X", but nothing more than "the majority approve of X." Hume's claim to an objective standard for moral valuation is interpreted by Broad then as a call for social statistics. If a given standard of moral values is approved of by the majority of people in a given society, then that standard qualifies as objective.

On the basis of Hume's position, however, something may be morally good if no one approves of it and even if everyone disapproves of it. Vice and virtue are not defined by Hume in terms of what people actually feel, but what a person would feel if he were to contemplate an action, character, or quality for what it is in a purely disinterested way. Far from being a case of majority sentiment, moral valuation in numbers alone is the exception and not the rule. Hume himself is quite clear about this aspect of his position, though Broad is but one of many who fails to credit him with requisite distinction between moral sentiment and sentiments from interest. Referring to this distinction, Hume says,

> It is true, those sentiments from interest and morals are apt to be confounded, and naturally run into one another. It seldom happens that we do not think an enemy vicious, and can distinguish betwixt his opposition to our interest and real villainy or baseness. But this hinders not but that the sentiments are in themselves distinct; and a man of temper and judgement may preserve himself from these illusions.[24]

"A man of temper and judgement" may preserve himself from the illusion of judging morally when he is in reality only judging from a partial or interested point of view, but the majority of men no doubt can never rise to such distinctions.

But the criterion of impartiality does not in itself explain much. We might be willing to grant that impartiality is a sufficient condition of objectivity in moral valuation, but not that impartiality is an attainable goal, especially within a framework of human sentiment. If there is no natural distinction between moral sentiment (pleasure) and other sentiments of interest, between the disinterested contemplation of moral character and the pleasure we get from a good bottle of wine, as Hume points out himself,[25] how can we recognize, much less achieve, an impartial point of view? Hume gives the only answer available to him, though one which is so far inconsistent with his better known position in Books I and II concerning the role of reason in conduct as to go either unnoticed or unappreciated. Hume's ultimate position in Book III is that the distinction between moral and other sorts of sentiment lies not in the nature of sentiment, but in the manner or mode of moral perception:

> . . .it is impossible we could ever converse together on any reasonable terms, were each of us to consider characters and persons only as they appear from his peculiar point of view. In order, therefore, to prevent those continual *contradictions* and arrive at a more *stable* judgement of things, we fix on some *steady* and *general* points of view, and always, in our thoughts, place ourselves in them, whatever may be our present situation. In like manner, external beauty is determined merely by pleasure; and it is evident a beautiful countenance cannot give so much pleasure, when seen at a distance of twenty paces, as when it is brought nearer us. We say not, however, that it appears less beautiful; because we know what effect it will have in such a position, and by that reflection we correct its momentary appearance.[26]

It is through reason or reflection that we draw the distinction between moral sentiment and mere pleasure, and in this respect, it is sentiment and not reason which is impotent. This is not to say, however, that moral distinctions are perceived by reason. Hume is not here taking exception to his original position that reason or reflection *alone* can never perceive vice and virtue or provide a motive for moral conduct. Rather, it is to say that reason is a necessary condition of moral valuation. No valuation is accepted as moral unless that valuation results from a general or disinterested point of view, and no such point of view can be acheived except through reflection.

Moral standards, then, have nothing essentially to do with the number of persons who are pleased or displeased by something, but with the manner in which, or the conditions under which, our pleasure or displeasure is felt. We may say, therefore, that reason or reflection and sentiment together provide a necessary, but neither one alone a sufficient, condition of moral valuation. Sentiment alone can never carry us beyond our own immediate perceptions, and though majority sentiment does provide us with a general standard, in no way does it provide us with a moral standard. And, on the other hand, reason alone would never be prompted to consider an object, impartially or otherwise, except as it is moved to do so by feeling. It is because we are naturally moved by characters, actions, and qualities in the first place that we seek in the second place to contemplate them from an impartial point of view.

Hume's view of objective or genuine moral judgment, then, refers to the exception and not the rule in a given society. It is not majority interest or attitude, but the conditions under which individuals, apart from personal interest and on the basis of understanding, morally judge that constitutes the standard of moral objectivity. And though our success according to such a standard will be varied and generally modest, a basis for reasonable debate and disagreement in moral matters is provided. We can not only discuss the question of impartiality in ourselves and others in the light of a greater understanding of own prejudices and interests, but we can point out to each other the inadequacy of our feelings in the light of new evidence. It is our reflective reason continually giving rise to new attitudes and sentiments and these in turn giving rise to new questions and concerns, which reflection alone can resolve, that constitutes the process of moral valuation for Hume.

At this point, we must guard ourselves against a commonly accepted implication. Hume's argument seems to imply that moral valuation involves the combination of two different functions, reflection and sentiment, such that the two are equally necessary, but logically distinct. Hume seems to be saying, at least at certain points in the *Treatise*, that moral value is strictly a matter of sentiment or feeling, and although reason or reflection does serve the necessary function of guiding and refining that feeling, it is nevertheless a secondary aspect of moral valuation. Daiches Raphael is but one of many contemporary philosophers who accepts such an interpretation. He even goes so far as to attribute to Hume a double theory of judgment.[27] Raphael distinguishes judgments concerning moral sentiment from judgments concerning conditions or fact. Such an interpretation, however, appears more reasonable and acceptable than it really is, not only because Hume misleadingly suggests it himself at times, but because contemporary moralists commonly accept the distinction between evaluative and descriptive judgment as the unquestionable basis of all moral theory. This distinction is in general agreement, for example, with the emotivist view that moral judgment involves a combination of two related but logically distinct activities, though not judgments. It is but a short step, then, to an interpretation of Hume in terms of emotivist ethics, interpreting moral judgment as description of fact and judgments of sentiment as expressions of feeling.

But this is not Hume's final position. Two basic problems force Hume to develop his theory in a different direction. On the basis of the above interpretation, Hume's theory cannot account successfully either for moral obligation or for the matter of objectivity in moral valuation. If descriptive judgments (statements) have one one job to perform and evaluative judgments another, how can we ever *justify* what we *feel* we *ought* to do? How, in other words, can our moral values be made to reflect our circumstances and *vice versa*? If our evaluative judgments serve only to express emotion, exhort, commend, recommend, etc. and if our descriptive judgments serve only to describe, identify, point out, etc., then how can one ever infer a statement of value from one of fact, an "ought" from an "is"? Or, to put the matter in yet another way, if moral value involves the *de facto* constitution and interests of man, how can we account for obligation within such a framework? Moreover, in a related manner, the problem of objectivity arises in an insoluble manner. If "reflection" is identified with "descriptive judgment" and "sentiment" with "expression of emotion," Hume is left not only with an unbridgeable gap between fact and value, but an inadequate basis for genuine moral debate and disagreement. For one can argue on the basis of the above interpretation of Hume that moral disagreements can be resolved only so far as they concern matters of fact; otherwise, one can only say *de gustibus non est disputandum*. "X is good" is reducible, in this respect, into the descriptive judgment "I have a feeling of approval on the contemplation of X" (objective, confirmable, and factual), on the one hand, and the evaluative expression of emotion or feeling (subjective and unconfirmable), on the other. But any attempt to translate or reduce or define the evaluative expression of emotion, i.e. "good," so that we may discuss and confirm our moral values objectively, involves a fallacy, i.e. the so-called "naturalistic fallacy." "Good," if definable at all, is only definable in terms of other evaluative (moral) concepts. As Strawson puts it, ". . .for every expression containing the words 'right' or 'good,' used in their ethical senses, it is always possible to find an expression with the same meaning, but containing, instead of these, the word 'ought.' The equivalences are various, and the variation subtle, but they are always to be found."[28] But the non-moral or descriptive equivalences of "good" or "ought" can never be found, since evaluation and description represent two fundamentally different categories of activity and consequently two different types of statement.

This position, however, is not in the final analysis representative of Hume, though it is representative of a major side of the *Treatise*. For example, what could be a more forceful and direct defense of the above position than Hume's conclusion that "Morality, therefore, is more properly felt than judged of."[29] The implication is obvious here that moral valuation in its primary or proper sense does not involve judgment (description) but only expression of feeling (evaluation). And elsewhere he points to a basic distinction between description and evaluation:

> . . .the understanding can neither justify nor condemn [feeling]. . .
> a passion must be accompany'd with some false judgment, in order
> to its being unreasonable; and even then 'tis not the passion, prop-
> erly speaking, which is unreasonable, but the judgment.[30]

But the major difficulty in trying to exhibit the inadequacy of the above interpretation of Hume lies not so much in the fact that Hume himself explicitly supports it at times, but in the fact that he qualifies and questions his general principles only indirectly as they fail to deal adequately with the problem at hand. For example, we saw in Chapter III above that Hume virtually contradicts in Book III his original view of the self in Book I of the *Treatise*. But the change from the view of the self as a "bundle of particulars," each absolutely separable and distinct,[31] to the view of the self as a whole or unity of which we always have a vivid impression,[32] is made with no comment or reconsideration of his original position. We saw also that Hume develops a new theory of definition and a fundamentally different view of the relationship between ideas and impressions, reason and sentiment, in order to deal more satisfactorily with moral experience. Yet, he at no time explicitly recognizes any basic change in his position. Consequently, it is only if we recognize the ultimate incompatibility between these parts of Books I and II which are based on analogies and models drawn from the physical sciences (Newtonian), on the one hand, and those parts of Books II and III which are based on analogies and models drawn from conduct, family, and so on (Hutchesonian), on the other, that we can appreciate the extent to which Hume's moral position is incompatible with his epistemology. And it is in his epistemology alone that the subordination of reason and the dichotomy of experience into impressions and ideas, relations of ideas and matters of fact, reason and sentiment, find what relevance and value they might have.

The biological and not the mechanical model is ultimately applicable to Hume's moral theory. Reason and sentiment are not two parts of a whole, but two aspects of a biological unity. I admit that such concepts are foreign to contemporary philosophical discussions, especially within the so-called analytic tradition, which is itself modelled largely on Lockean and Humean epistemology, and therefore may appear forced for the sake of argument. But I mean nothing extravagant or unreasonable here. I mean only that Hume must ultimately be viewed within the tradition of naturalism which extends back to the greatest naturalist of all, Aristotle. It is in Aristotle that custom, training, reason, and sentiment come together to produce virtue and goodness in such a way that part-whole analysis is wholly inapplicable. Whether we call such a unity "biological" or "organic" or "dynamic" or whatever matters little. It is clear, however, that in respect to such a unity (and every character or personality in fact represents such a unity) it is only by violating the naturalness of experience that we can isolate the rational from the sentimental, educational, and customary qualities. And Hume himself admits, in the one section of the *Treatise* where he considers the specifically moral or "calm" passions, that the distinction between reflection and passion, when those passions are moral ones, is an impossible one to draw on the basis of experience alone:

> Reason, for instance, exerts itself without producing any sensible emotion. . . Hence it proceeds, that every action of the mind, which operates with the same calmness and tranquility, is confounded with reason. . .[33]

If it is impossible to distinguish reflection from sentiment during the process of genuine moral valuation, then it is only on the basis of theory that the distinction can be drawn, if at all. And once again, if we recognize the fact that the theoretical arguments which are offered by Hume to support the view that "reason is perfectly inert"[34] are based on epistemological assumptions which do not apply to his moral theory, we can go on to recognize the practical and primary role that Hume ultimately does assign to reflection in moral valuation. In fact, it is in this section on the calm passions that Hume is most direct in identifying moral action with an Aristotelian blend of reflection, sentiment, and training. There are statements, for example, where he argues that to be determined by a calm passion, i.e. morally, is to be determined by "a settled principle of action" or "the predominant inclination of the soul."[35] Moreover, the distinction between the "calm" and "violent" passions is intended by Hume to exhibit what is meant by reasonable conduct:

> Men often counteract a violent passion in prosecution of their own interests and designs; it is not, therefore, the present uneasiness alone which determines them.[36]

This is a function which Hume later assigns to reflective judgment. In fact, he goes on to say that to have a calm passion is to give "preference to whatever is in itself preferable,"[37] a function he also later assigns to reflection. He says further that the calm passions are "founded on a distant view."[38] It would indeed be remarkable if all calm or *moral* passions were founded on a distant view by accident. Clearly, Hume is saying that we take this distant view in order to ensure, or attempt to ensure, the reasonableness—the justness, rightness, or goodness—of our attitudes and judgments. It is no wonder, then, that Hume cannot in the final analysis distinguish reason and sentiment in genuine moral conduct.

The point, then, is that to have a morality at all requires an understanding of human conduct from a number of basic points of view: natural as well as social behavior, personality as well as politics, needs as well as desires. The "distant view," to "give preference to what is in itself preferable," and to " corroborate by reflection and second by resolution,"[39] are operations which depend equally upon sentiment and reflection and which can only be successful from a standpoint of knowledge and understanding of fact: judgment and understanding provide a corrective and thereby objective framework for the otherwise subjective affections. Our inquiries into the nature of human experience and conduct are made with the intention of arriving at those kinds of "peculiar" feelings we call moral approval, and the understanding we arrive at is the necessary condition of moral valuation, not in the sense that understanding causes or gives rise to sentiment, but in the sense that understanding gives rise to *approval*. Approval is sentiment, but sentiment whose nature is self-consciously reflected. This self-conscious sentiment or approval is so far from being mere sentiment alone that we often mistake it for reason, for indeed, in the area of morality, it serves an identical function. This in fact is Hume's position in Book III:

> Here we are contented with saying, that reason requires such an impartial conduct, but that it is seldom we can bring ourselves to it, and that our passions do not readily follow the determination of our judgement. This language will be easily understood, if we consider what we formerly said concerning that *reason* which is

able to oppose our passion; and which we have found to be nothing but a general calm determination of the passions, founded on some distant view or reflexion.[40]

Hume is saying here in one statement both that reason does, though seldom unfortunately, determine our passions and that what we take to be reason in moral valuation and "calm" passions are identical. Hume has gone in the *Treatise* from the theoretical claim that reason can never operate practically to the merely verbal claim that reason ought really to be called "reflective passion" in the area of morality. We cannot in all fairness accept this new position as an argument against reason, for it does not undermine the practical role of reason, but merely gives it another name.

In this respect, Hume can be viewed as a forerunner of Dewey's comprehensive analysis of nature, conduct, and art, where the methods employed are both empirical and naturalistic, for, as Dewey observes, "culture" is but a synonym for "reflective experience," and reflective experience is itself an organic blend of the instrumental and the given. Similarly, we can say that morality is for Hume a synonym for reflective experience, for, like Dewey, Hume ultimately acknowledges the organic unity of experience by employing an empirical and naturalistic methodology in moral enquiry modelled not on the mechanistic naturalism of Newton, but the humanistic naturalism of Hutcheson and Shaftesbury. And this view of the nature of practical reason in moral valuation I take to be Hume's ultimate position. It is, however, a position so incompatible with the view of reason generally implied in Books I and II as to contradict it directly. But we cannot escape the conclusion of Book III that moral valuation, though never wholly reducible to the flow or giveness of human experience, cannot be done in isolation from it. This, after all, is just one way of expressing the fundamental distinction between the moral and the formal or physical sciences.

On the basis of the foregoing analysis the question raised in Chapter IV concerning the relationship between Is and Ought, fact and value, can be answered now. It will be recalled that

All morality depends upon our sentiments; and when any action or quality of the mind pleases us *after a certain manner,* we say it is virtuous; and when the neglect or non-performance of it displeases us *after a like manner,* we say that we lie under an obligation to perform it.[41]

Moral obligations are related to the thought of moral acts or, more properly, to the sentiments of which we morally approve and associate with those acts. To say that we are morally obliged then, is to say that we are moved to do those acts whose associated sentiments morally please us and whose neglect or non-performance would therefore displease us. Our moral obligations thus are theoretically commensurate with our moral virtues, since any moral virtue can be considered in theory from the point of view of its non-performance. To determine our moral values, then, is tantamount to determining our moral obligations. Likewise, the determination of fact or the question of empirical judgment is as fundamental to moral obligation as to moral approval in general: "an alteration. . .in the temper and circumstances of mankind, would entirely alter our duties and obligations."[42] The relationship between Is and Ought is therefore as intimate as that between sentiment and will, the qualification being that the moral ought is only prompted by a sentiment *after a certain manner,* in other words, a sentiment of *moral* approval.

The union between reason and sentiment is even clearer in Hume's treatment of the so-called "artificial virtues." According to Hume the criterion of justification of our moral concepts and institutions is to be found in the origins of these concepts and institutions in the principles of human nature and the practical concerns of man. But some of our moral concepts and institutions, for example, justice, though serving an obvious practical function in society, seem not to be founded on human nature. Hume, in fact, begins his discussion of the "artificial" virtues by posing this problem:

> . . .our sense of every kind of virtue is not natural; but that there
> are some virtues, that produce pleasure and approbation by means
> of an artifice or contrivance, which arises from the circumstances
> and necessity of mankind. Of this kind I assert *justice* to be. . .[43]

We have, Hume points out, motives to keep promises and to respect laws and property. Yet, it seems evident that we have no "natural" desires to do so. Our strongest instinct is self-love, "But 'tis certain, that self-love, when it acts at its liberty, instead of engaging us to honest actions, is the source of all injustice and violence."[44] Nor, Hume argues, is there any one general sentiment, such as the love of mankind, through which we might trace the origins of justice:

> In general, it may be affirm'd, that there is no such passion in
> human minds, as the love of mankind, merely as such, independent
> of personal qualities, of services, or of relation to ourself.[45]

But even our concern and interest in those of special "relation to ourself," cannot account for motive of justice, since justice is often contrary to our interests and the interests of those near us. Hume says,

> 'Tis true, there is no human, and indeed no sensible, creature,
> whose happiness or misery does not, in some measure, affect us,
> when brought near to us, and represented in lively colours; But
> this proceeds merely from sympathy, and is no proof of such a
> universal affection to mankind. Since this concern extends itself
> beyond our own species.[46]

If, therefore, neither our regard for our own interests and of those near to us not "public benevolence," or the "love of mankind," can serve as the original motive to justice, how can Hume account for this motive within the general framework of "human nature" and "interest?" Hume's answer to this question is that many of our social virtues and concerns derive from the natural principles of human nature *indirectly.* Justice, for example, finds its immediate, or direct, motive in *reason,* not in the natural passions. However, Hume does not give to reason here the sort of a priori basis that Moore has in mind. The motive to justice is not a product of our "intuition" or "reflective judgment" in Moore's sense of that term. Hume is careful to emphasize that "...the sense of justice is not founded on reason, or on the discovery of certain connexions and relations of ideas, which are eternal, immutable, and universally obligatory."[47] According to Hume, reason can have an influence on our conduct in only two ways:

> Either when it excites a passion by informing us of the existence of something which is a proper object of it; or when it discovers the connexion of causes and effects, so as to afford us means of exerting any passion.[48]

It is in this latter sense in which Hume regards justice as founded on reason. Reason points out *means* to *ends,* and justice is just one of those *means,* or "artifices," to a "natural" end. Hume's reasoning is briefly that the many instinctive, or "natural," desires of man for his happiness and pleasures find their fulfillment in society. In order to live in society, however, we must behave in ways which often run directly contrary to our selfish interests. Reason, therefore, operates to create the means, the "artifice," through which our "natural" interests can best be accommodated. It is this respect that Hume says,

> In vain shou'd we expect to find, in *uncultivated nature,* a remedy to this inconvenience; or hope for any inartificial principle of the human mind, which might controul those partial affections, and make us overcome the temptations arising from our circumstances. The idea of justice can never serve to this purpose, or be taken for a natural principle...[49]

But though justice cannot be identified with either a "natural" principle of human nature or with the "natural" interests of man, it nevertheless *serves* both a "natural" sentiment (self-love) and the "social" interests of man (the harmonious pursuit of individual interest). Hume's analysis of our idea of justice, then, has taken us from its relationship to human nature to its relationship to social utility, from a concern with *origins* to a concern with *results.* And any program which fails to account for our moral ideas in both these respects is fundamentally inadequate.

Is Hume's analysis of Justice "objective"?

Hume's analysis is *not* objective in Moore's sense of that term; Hume is not concerned to give the *one* correct verbal and conceptual definition of justice. Justice is a dynamic, changing social concept, according to Hume, and is therefore not susceptible to the sort of "real" definition and analysis of *Principia Ethica.* For just as "an alteration in the temper and circumstances of mankind, would entirely alter our duties and obligations,"[50] according to Hume, so also would such an alteration influence the specific content of our idea of justice. Consequently, the question whether a given view of justice is "correct," is dependent upon the more basic question concerning the permanent features of human nature and the interests of man. To the extent that our definitions and analyses relate to, and draw upon, human nature and interest, to that extent they can be said to be objective and relevant. This, indeed, is the final word of the *Treatise:*

> Most of the inventions of men are subject to change. They depend
> upon humour and caprice. They have a vogue for a time, and then
> sink into oblivion. It may, perhaps, be apprehended, that if justice
> were allow'd to be a human invention, it must be plac'd on the
> same footing. But the cases are widely different. The interest, on
> which justice is founded, is the greatest imaginable, and extends to
> all times and places. It cannot possibly be serv'd by any other in-
> vention. It is obvious, and discovers itself on the very first forma-
> tion of society. All these causes render the rules of justice stedfast
> and immutable, at least, as immutable as human nature. And if
> they were founded on original instincts, cou'd they have any great-
> er stability?[51]

As moral philosophers, if we can determine the principles of human nature and
the human interests that must be served, we can, to that extent, proceed on an
objective basis.

Moore's program for moral philosophy

In the Preface to *Principia Ethica,* Moore draws the outlines of his own
view of the various relationships between the broad questions of the nature and
proper object of ethical theory. He begins with the promising words,

> It appears to me that in Ethics, as in all other philosophical studies,
> the difficulties and disagreements, of which its history is full, are
> mainly due to a very simple cause: namely to the attempt to an-
> swer questions, without first discovering precisely *what* question it
> is which you desire to answer.[52]

And he goes on to suggest that by recognizing and answering the "right" questions in ethics, "many of the most glaring difficulties and disagreements in
philosophy would disappear."[53]

What are the "right" questions, then, according to Moore? They are
(1) What kind of things ought to exist for their own sakes? (2) What kind of
actions ought we to perform? and (3) What is the nature of the evidence, by
which alone any ethical proposition can be proved or disproved, confirmed or
rendered doubtful?[54] In respect to (1), that is, questions of ultimate value,
Moore holds that "no relevant evidence whatever can be adduced: from no
other truth, except themselves alone, can it be inferred that they are either true
or false.[55] In other words, Moore sees no real connection between our ultimate
values and beliefs, on the one side, and what we naturally regard as *evidence* for
holding them, on the other, between the premises of our moral reasoning and
our moral experience, between theory and practice. Indeed, the desire to imple-
ment such an ethical program is expressed by Moore to be the main object of
Principia Ethica:

> I have endeavoured to write 'Prolegomena to any future Ethics
> that can possibly pretend to be scientific.' In other words, I have
> endeavoured to discover what are the fundamental principles of
> ethical reasoning, and the establishment of these principles, *rather*

than any conclusions which may be attained by their use, may be regarded as my main object.[56] (Emphasis mine)

This distinction between "principles," or theory, and practice is an interesting and significant one. It poses an issue which is at the heart of ethical theory. Albert William Levi expresses it as follows:

For there is, I think, a crucial point of theory, perhaps even of logic, at stake here also. For between the 'fundamental principles of moral reasoning' and 'the conclusions which may be attained by their use' there is, if not perhaps a relation of strict entailment, at least an extremely close and an extremely important relation. Particularly when these fundamental principles of moral reasoning have definitely *not* been previously established on independent grounds, then attention to the conclusions which may be attained by their use *has* become relevant to the unsettled question of whether they are indeed both fundamental and valid as principles of reasoning.[57]

The "point of theory" to which Levi alludes is whether moral theory is to draw upon the store of human experience, to reflect and generalize it, and ultimately, to prove its own worth and justification by directing it, or whether moral theory can be developed independently of experience and practice and can find its justification internally, within its own framework of "self-evident" principles. This is the crucial issue which separates Hume and Moore in ethics, and which faces every moral philosopher today. Perhaps, indeed, it has been the fundamental issue of ethics throughout the history of ethical theory, for an answer to it appears to lead the theorist in either of two irreconcilable directions.

Moore is not the first ethical theorist to turn his back, in his formal analysis of ethical terms, on the relevance to their meaning of actual practice. This prejudice finds deep roots in Kant's ethics, and Plato suggests such a solution a number of times and in a variety of ways. I cannot help but see a deep connection between Socrates' insistence in the *Meno* on finding precisely what "virtue" means, or stands for, and Moore's "right question-right answer" thinking in ethics and his narrow view of goodness to the effect that it is a constant, independent, intuitable entity, simple and beautiful to those of us reflective enough to recognize it.

Such an orientation contributes much to Moore's extravagant and false view of previous ethical theories as resting on a common fallacy; to the parallel misinterpretation and misunderstanding which sees in those same theories an attempt to give a specific definition of goodness, in the sense of finding the specific thing or concept with which it can properly be identified; and ultimately to the unphilosophical and naive view of goodness as being "good and that is the end of the matter."[58] For this restricted view of goodness and the fundamental questions of ethics not only dominates Moore's critical arguments and his historical interpretations, but his positive moral theory as well.

I have considered the negative arguments of Chapter I of *Principia Ethica* and the question of their historical relevance. We tried to show not only that the Naturalistic Fallacy is false on its own grounds, but that it is irrelevant to Hume's moral theory. I think it desirable now to look briefly at some of Moore's positive results. Perhaps the strongest evidence for rejecting Moore's positive program for moral philosophy lies in the nature of his results.

It is rarely a topic of conversation among Moore's followers today, but it is clear that to Moore, his ethical program finds its culmination and ultimate justification in the "wisdom" of Chapter VI of *Principia Ethica*, "The Ideal." The heart of "The Ideal" is,

> If, now, we use this method of absolute isolation, and guard against these errors, it appears that the question we have to answer is far less difficult than the controversies of Ethics might have led us to expect. Indeed, once the meaning of the question is clearly under- stood, the answer to it, in its main outlines, appears to be obvious, that it runs the risk of seeming to be a platitude. By far the most valuable things, which we know or can imagine, are certain states of consciousness, which may be roughly described as the pleasures of human intercourse and the enjoyment of beautiful objects. . . This simple truth may, indeed, be said to be universally recognized. What has *not* been recognized is that it is the ultimate and funda- mental truth of Moral Philosophy.[59]

One could simply accept the above as the Bloomsbury Manifesto, if it were not for Moore's insistence that his results are "universally recognized" and the "fundamental truth of Moral Philosophy." In fact, Moore even goes on to claim,

> Nor. . .does it appear probable that anyone will think that any- thing else has *nearly* so great a value as the things which are in- cluded under these two heads.[60]

Does Moore really believe, and expect us to believe, that the "pleasures of human intercourse" are "by far the most valuable" when compared, for exam- ple, to the "pleasures of human solitude"? or, "the enjoyment of beautiful objects" when compared to "the creation of beautiful objects"?[61]

To be sure, there is no simple way to decide these matters. But the im- portant point is that these questions concerning specific goods and bads are not the primary questions of ethical philosophy. The "method of absolute isola- tion" is perhaps the only method of philosophizing which can possibly give to Moore's results some sense of universal significance. But when brought into the light of human conduct and experience, out of isolation, so to speak, these questions are seen to presuppose far more comprehensive and meaningful ones. It is in this important and basic respect that Hume's ethical program towards the discovery of principles for actual utilization and application is justified and Moore's program must be rejected.

Why talking about the nature of moral argument is relevant to moral discourse, while defining "good" as an isolated quality is not.

"The Ideal" clearly exhibits Moore's preoccupation with "ultimate" moral truths:

> the *consciousness* of beauty. . .is the ultimate and fundamental
> truth of Moral Philosophy. . .the *raison d'etre* of virtue. . .the ulti-
> mate end of human action and the sole criterion of social prog-
> ress. . .[62]

Moore wants to avoid the "error. . .which consists in supposing that what seems absolutely necessary here and now, for the existence of anything good. . .is therefore good in itself."[63] In a word, Moore is deeply opposed to the possibility that our moral values are relative, a possibility which to Moore would destroy the autonomy of ethics. If values are ultimate, then they are independent of the changing, indefinite circumstances of man.

But is this a justified concern? It is a fact of existence that our circumstances change and that we must constantly reassess our values and institutions. This seems to me, however, to be a desirable state of affairs, if only because it gives our institutions of learning a central purpose in society and a moral basis on which to stand. As Professor Charles Frankel expresses this view,

> Values. . .are the expressions of human preference, and have a psy-
> chological and social setting and an historical career. If there are
> any moral standards. . .it is human beings who make them. If there
> is any meaning to history, it is human beings who put it there.[64]

This means, one admits, that values are not "ultimate," if one has in mind the sort of "isolatable" static truths of "The Ideal." But it does not mean that our values and moral considerations must therefore lack *autonomy and objectivity*. Morality is autonomous; this is a result of logical analysis—not of complex verbal definitions, but of the *facts* of moral experience. *Moral distinctions* are facts, and it is the analysis and recognition of these facts which distinguishes morality from other domains. Moreover, the crucial issue for moral philosophy is not between "ultimate" and "relative" values. It concerns rather the problem of determining the method best suited to provide us with objective and relevant results. We reject Moore's program for moral philosophy, not because his results are subjective and arbitrary, which they clearly are, but because his program itself necessarily produces such results. Rather than provide answers to our moral questions, or even any basis for an eventual solution, Moore's use of "reflective judgment" in conjunction with "the method of absolute isolation" cuts off speculation at its source. Hume is well aware of the consequences of accepting such a position:

> Shall we, then, establish it for a general maxim, that no refin'd or
> elaborate reasoning is ever to be receiv'd? Consider well the conse-
> quences of such a principle. By this means you cut off entirely all
> science and philosophy: You proceed upon one singular quality of
> the imagination, and by a parity of reason must embrace all of
> them: And you expressly contradict yourself; since this maxim
> must be built on the preceding reasoning, which will be allow'd to
> be sufficiently refin'd and metaphysical.[65]

"Reflective judgment," or "intuition," is a "parity of reason," because we must in the last analysis "embrace" each and every one of its conclusions.[66]

Hume is making here a broad and significant point about ethical enquiry, as well. Hume is making the point that ethical enquiry must combine the theoretical and the practical, the speculative and the common. Mere reliance on either common sense, on the one hand, or theoretical reasoning, on the other, will always result in a "parity of reason." If certain practical matters suggest to us a number of theoretical or philosophical problems, as our moral judgments and actions do, then we must look outside the theoretical, to the practical origins of our problems, in order both to orient and guide our speculations and eventually to evaluate their merit.

Whether our theoretical speculations lead us to the principle of the association of ideas and the mechanism of sympathy, as in the *Treatise,* or to extended benevolence, as in the *Enquiry,* is secondary. Our analyses of human conduct in whatever specific domain will naturally change with the development of the whole body of human knowledge. But the need to wed our practical considerations with our theoretical speculations is unqualified and basic in a practical or partially applied area such as ethics. And we cannot wed our theory with our practice unless we develop our theory, our philosophical program, in the light of our practices. Our moral discourse should shape our moral theory; our program should result from our needs and interests. It is only under these conditions that we can reasonably expect our conclusions to be adequate and "objective."

Once this is recognized and accepted, the question whether Moore's position in ethics is reasonable or unreasonable, valid, or invalid, relevant or irrelevant, is answered. Indeed, anyone who sees the answers to our deepest concerns of moral conduct lying in the direction of "intuition" and "absolute isolation," abandons the road of traditional moral enquiry for the self-enclosed activity of verbal clarification and intuitive judgment. One should be cautious when generalizing about the history of twentieth century ethics, but it is difficult not to see in Moore's approach the reflections of that mentality which, in numbers alone, seems to represent our times and which sees a virtue in the professional, the pedantic, the verbal, and the merely logical.

[1]*Principia*, p. 187.

[2]Where Moore employs the terms "goodness," Hume speaks of "moral good and evil" (*Treatise*, p. 456), "virtue and vice," (*Ibid.*, p. 470), and "sentiment of blame or approbation" (*Ibid.*, p. 291).

[3]*Treatise*, p. 618.

[4]*Ibid.*, p. 470.

[5]*Ibid.*, p. 415.

[6]*Ibid.*, p. 458.

[7]*Ibid.*, p. 493.

[8]*Ibid.*, p. 418.

[9]*Ibid.*, p. 469-70. (Italics mine.)

[10]*Ibid.*, p. 470.

[11]*Ibid.*, p. 517.

[12]*Ibid.*, p. 415.

[13]*Ibid.*, p. 469.

[14]C. D. Broad, *Five Types of Ethical Theory,* London, Kegan Paul, Trench, Trubner & Co. LTD, p. 85.

[15]*Ibid.*, p. 115.

[16]See Rachael Kydd's excellent work, *Reason and Conduct in Hume's Treatise,* for a detailed analysis of the changing roles of reason in the *Treatise.*

[17]*Treatise*, p. 469.

[18]*Ibid.*, p. 472.

[19]*Ibid.*, p. 582.

[20]*Ibid.*, p. 472.

[21]*Ibid.*, p. 591.

[22]*Ibid.*, p. 472.

[23]*Ibid.*, p. 268.

[24]*Ibid.*, p. 472.

[25]*Ibid.*, p. 472.

[26]*Ibid.*, pp. 581-82.

[27]Daiches D. Raphael, *The Moral Sense,* London, Oxford University Press, 1947.

[28]P. F. Strawson, "Ethical Intuitionism," *Philosophy,* 1949, p. 30.

[29]*Treatise*, p. 470.

[30]*Ibid.*, p. 416.

[31]*Ibid.*, pp. 207 and 251 ff.

[32]*Ibid.*, p. 317.

[33]*Ibid.*, p. 417.

[34]*Ibid.*,

34*Ibid.*, p. 458.

35*Ibid.*, p. 419.

36*Ibid.*, p. 418.

37*Ibid.*, p. 536.

38*Ibid.*, p. 583.

39*Ibid.*, p. 437.

40*Ibid.*, p. 583.

41*Ibid.*, p. 517.

42*Ibid.*, p. 496.

43*Ibid.*, p. 477.

44*Ibid.*, p. 480.

45*Ibid.*, p. 481.

46*Ibid.*, p. 481.

47*Ibid.*, p. 496.

48*Ibid.*, p. 459.

49*Ibid.*, p. 488.

50*Ibid.*, p. 496.

51*Ibid.*, p. 620.

52*Principia*, p. vii.

53*Ibid.*, p. vii.

54*Ibid.*, p. viii.

55*Ibid.*, p. viii.

56*Ibid.*, p. ix.

57Albert William Levi, "The Trouble with Ethics: Values, Method, and the Search for Moral Norms," *Mind*, vol. 70, 1961, p. 206.

58*Principia*, p. 6.

59*Ibid.*, pp. 188-189.

60*Ibid.*, pp. 88-89.

61These examples are borrowed from Albert William Levi's essay, "The Trouble with Ethics: Values, Method, and the Search for Moral Norms," *Mind*, vol. 70, 1961, pp. 212-213.

62*Principia*, p. 189.

63*Ibid.*, p. 189.

64Charles Frankel, *The Case For Modern Man*, Boston, Press, 1966, p. 56.

65*Treatise*, p. 268.

66Common sense, of course, is equally a "parity of reason." But Moore is not, as many believe, an advocate of "common sense" in ethics. He is as little representative of the wisdom and tastes of the "common man" as is the Bloomsbury Group of the wisdom and tastes of Barnaby Square.

CHAPTER VI

Conclusion

There are two sides to G. E. Moore, paralleling the two main themes in his philosophy. Each side represents an outlook, a style of thought, as well as a philosophical commitment. This book has been concerned mainly with the commitments, the arguments, as it were. On the one hand, Moore appeals to "common sense" (ordinary language), as in his view of meaning and the function of analysis, and, on the other hand, logical-linguistic devices, as in his "naturalistic fallacy" argument. The first is the argument that if a philosophical statement runs counter to common sense, it is, at least to that extent, mistaken. Ordinary language or common sense is held to be a paradigm of certainty and meaning, while analysis holds a secondary, philosophical function. The second is the argument that the realm of ethical value is separate from the "natural" world and that any attempt to define one in terms of the other is doomed to failure: the ethical cannot be reduced to the nonethical. In *Principia Ethica* the two came together to form the substance and appeal of that work and are consequently historically as well as philosophically interesting.

These themes parallel the major historical effects of Moore's thought.

103

They provide a foundation and connecting link for a number of closely related ethical theories, what can loosely be called a tradition. What is meant by a tradition here is a common set of assumptions and attitudes, a general agreement as to the main problems, an identifiable way, in short, of going about ethical enquiry. Moore provides an attitude and approach to ethical enquiry and towards traditional interest theories that inevitably leads to ethical intuitionism in his own work and subsequently to ethical emotivism and to the group of fundamental mistakes and misconceptions that Ayer and Stevenson, as examples, have so remarkably popularized.

The short history of twentieth century ethics is somewhat intriguing, especially the question how so many seemingly incompatible ethical theories find their sources in the same work, *Principia Ethica.* These questions, however, have been answered only by implication in this work, by exhibiting Moore's doctrine in detail, his method and general approach to philosophy and criticism, and by emphasizing the incompatible elements to be found there. For what has been of particular interest to me here and what forms the core of my work is not the historical question, nor even Moore's positive ethical theory, but his negative contention that all naturalistic ethical theories commit certain fundamental mistakes. My object has been to focus on this negative contention, determine its relationship to Moore's general position, and evaluate its force in respect to Hume's position.

However, Hume and Moore clash on personal and social values as well as on those strictly philosophical matters which have been our main concern. These less substantive issues, those of outlook and style of thought, offer us, moreover, a further reason for seeing in Hume the most representative of Moore's opponents and a pointed and personal summary of their philosophical differences. For it is only recently that we have come to see (and accept) a general divorce in philosophy between a man's professional and personal views, between the logical structure of his argument and the broad store of his personal commitment. Fortunately, both Hume and Moore are quite open and confident in regarding their own philosophies as expressions, and as philosophical examinations, of their personal views. The one reflects and draws upon the other.

But there is a further reason for considering the informal qualities of a philosopher's thought. The majority of people who come in contact with philosophy are not professional teachers of the subject, but students. It is the student who is more influenced by the general ethos of the teaching than by the philosophical subtleties of argument. In short, the informal, personal picture would serve a purpose, even if it were different from the more esoteric one. But in this case, the two are remarkably comparable.

G. E. Moore writes in his autobiography,

I do not think that the world or the sciences would ever have suggested to me any philosophical problems. What has suggested philosophical problems to me is things which other philosophers have said about the world of sciences.[1]

104

Ironically, this admission of naivete, so obviously unphilosophical and uncritical, marks a turning point in the history of modern philosophy. In this attitude, together with a number of basic philosophical assumptions also to be found in Moore's writings, can be traced the origins of what has come to be called the "linguistic school of philosophy." Moore's is the view that we begin with intellectual innocence, merely and naturally *using* language, without puzzling about it and hence without puzzling philosophically about the world. This stage has been humorously and pointedly compared to the happy stage in the life of a centipede "when it just wanders about using its legs but unworried by them."[2] Moore's "philosophy of common sense" says that it is not and cannot be the task of philosophy to challenge or assess the claims of common sense, but that its task is merely to clarify what is meant by those claims. He says in his famous essay, "A Defense of Common Sense,"

> I am not at all sceptical as to the *truth* of such propositions as "The earth has existed for many years past', 'Many human bodies have each lived for many years upon it', i.e., propositions which assert the existence of material things: on the contrary, I hold that we all know, with certainty, many such propositions to be true. But I am very sceptical as to what, in certain respects, the correct *analysis* of such propositions is"[3]

The above quote is a clear instance of the tension existing between the two main themes in Moore's thought. He seems never to have been struck by the oddness of claiming both that certain propositions are known with certainty (the appeal to common sense) and, at the same time, that these same propositions are in need of clarification (the appeal to logical-linguistic devices or *philosophy*). Indeed, if we interpret the "Philosophy of common sense" as saying that a term cannot be identified falsely with its characteristic application, then "common sense" systematically commits the naturalistic fallacy in moral experience, where the fallacy is in ever identifying a moral term, e.g. "good", with its characteristic application.[4] In other words, Moore is never quite certain as to the role, if any, that philosophy is to play, whether it is to correct the abuses of philosophy or those of common sense. He says in his essay, "A Defense of Common Sense," referring to a number of "common sense" examples,

> . . .if they are features in the Common Sense view of the world (whether 'we' know this is not), it follows that they are true. . .[5]

Yet in *Principia Ethica,* though he gives token recognition to common sense, Moore views "meaning" and "knowing" in terms of intuition and has no qualms about enunciating a paradox or wholly unusual contention where his theory demands it.

But my criticisms of Moore run deeper than mere ambivalence on his part. I see in Moore's attitude an implicit, and at times, explicit, criticism of all moral and intellectual inquisitiveness. His view is the reversal of our traditional view that philosophy is preoccupation with the deeper intellectual, emotional, and moral issues. Indeed, Moore would have us believe that we *ought not* to be concerned with such matters in the daily course of our lives—after all, it was a handful of verbal peculiarities that brought Moore to philosophy in the first place.

Moore says in *Principia Ethica* by way of pointing out the significance and force of his arguments in that book for society and the guidance of one's life:

> The individual can therefore be confidently recommended *always* to conform to rules which are both generally useful and generally practised.[6]

And,

> . . .though we may be sure that there are cases where the rule should be broken, *we can never know which those cases are,* (we) ought, therefore, never to break it.[7] (Emphasis mine.)

He even goes on to say,

> It is undoubtedly well to punish a man, who has done an action, right in his case but generally wrong, even if his example would not be likely to have a dangerous effect.[8]

These are rather extraordinary things for a person to say *if* that person sees in his work some practical value, some bearing on the social question—but Moore does not:

> . . .it seems doubtful whether Ethics can establish the utility of any rules other than those generally practised. But its inability to do so is fortunately of little practical moment. The question whether the general observance of a rule not generally observed, would or would not be desirable, cannot much affect the question how any individual ought to act; since, on the one hand, the fact that its general observance would be useful could, in any case, give him no reason to conclude that he himself ought to observe it, in the absence of such general observance.[9]

While Hume, and Bentham and Mill after him, are trying to provide a philosophical support for certain changes in social rules and outlook, "trying to put the discussion of morals and politics on an objective and public basis," as Charles Frankel has put it,[10] Moore is little concerned about this aspect of moral enquiry, believing that "its inability to do so is fortunately of little practical moment." The discrepancy between the promise, "to discover the fundamental principles of ethical reasoning,"[11] and the performance of Moore's theory, providing an Ethics of no practical value, is startling. And though it is our present task to analyze the formal, ethical argument in Moore, his attitude and general social outlook serve, nevertheless, to provide a clear framework in which his argument is expressed.

The references in contemporary philosophical texts are too numerous to cite where Moore is viewed as the significant step in the sober return to Hume's careful and clear philosophizing. This view is only superficially true. Hume does consider at a number of points in the *Treatise* the alternative of embracing the obvious claims of common sense, much for the same reasons that Moore gives:

> I dine, I play a game of back-gammon, I converse, and am merry

with my friends; and when after three or four hours' amusement,
I wou'd return to these speculations, they appear so cold, and
strain'd, and ridiculous, that I cannot find in my heart to enter
into them any farther.[12]

Philosophy, as Moore suggests, seems to exist for its own peculiar paradoxical
reasons. But Hume clearly rejects this view. He says,

Consider well the consequences of such a principle. By this means
you cut off entirely all science and philosophy: You proceed upon
one singular quality of the imagination, and by a parity of reasoning must embrace all of them: And you expressly contradict your-
self; since this maxim must be built on the preceding reasoning,
which will be allow'd to be sufficiently refin'd and metaphysical.[13]

In other words, Hume rejects any *standard* of ordinary experience, though its
claims are admittedly "more easy and natural."[14] "By a parity of reasoning",
by the restriction of belief to "one singular quality of the imagination" (ordinary language), ordinary language or common sense becomes no standard at all.
One must embrace too much. And Hume is quite aware of the ultimate consequences of such a position, however much contemporary criticism wants to
credit Wittgenstein with a novel insight: for in order to erect a standard of common sense, one must build on reasoning which is "sufficiently refin'd and
metaphysical," and thus one must violate common sense itself. In other words,
the choice of common sense as a standard is not an arbitrary one; it entails a
philosophical commitment.

In short, Hume does feel doubt and uncertainty concerning the common
course of life, where Moore does not. Where the origin of philosophical puzzle-
ment is for Moore the incidental result of having been exposed to the "odd"
statements of other philosophers, for Hume it is,

. . .a curiosity to be acquainted with the principles of moral good
and evil, the nature and foundation of government, and the cause
of those several passions and inclinations, which actuate and govern
me. I am uneasy to think I approve of one object, and disapprove
of another; call one thing beautiful, and another deform'd; decide
concerning truth and falshood, reason and folly, without knowing
upon what principles I proceed.[15]

Where Moore considers moral enquiry to have little practical value, Hume views
it as a means to satisfy his ". . .ambition. . .of contributing to the instruction of
mankind, and of acquiring a name by my inventions and discoveries."[16] And
most importantly, where to Moore the question,

. . .how 'good' is to be defined, is the most fundamental question
in all Ethics[17]

and where in order to obtain experimentally

. . .a correct answer to the question 'What is good in itself?' we
must consider what value things would have if they existed absolutely by themselves,[18]

Hume has this to say,

Moral philosophy has, indeed, this peculiar disadvantage, which is not found in natural, that in collecting its experiments, it cannot make them purposely, with premeditation. . . But should I endeavour to clear up after the same manner any doubt in moral philosophy, by placing myself in the same case with that which I consider, 'tis evident this reflection and premeditation would so disturb the operation of my natural principles, as must render it impossible to form any just conclusion from the phaenomenon. We must therefore glean up our experiments in this science from a cautious observation of human life, and take them as they appear in the common course of the world, by men's behaviour in company, in affairs, and in their pleasures.[19]

The idea, then, that Moore is in some notable sense a restoration of Humean sanity or that Moore can be classed in that British tradition of which Hume is so representative is a false one. The separation of "belief" and "philosophy", however subtle its manner, is quite foreign to that tradition. The basic orientations of these two thinkers, both in personal outlook and philosophical argument, run counter to one another, and in many ways, their controversy is the one facing contemporary philosophy today.

Moral philosophy today begins with the assumption, due in large part to Moore's influence, that there exists a logical dichotomy between value and fact, between our attitude toward the world and the world itself, and that this gap represents the major barrier against any ethics based on actual interest and experience. But even to those theorists who find such a dichotomy unacceptable or unpalatable, the task of moral philosophy has become as well one of finding the logical model for acceptable inferences from fact to value, from Is to Ought. Indeed, underlying Moore's Naturalistic Fallacy claim is the view of the history of ethical theory as a series of attempts to define goodness, i.e. close the gap between fact and value, by finding the one property or properties of things with which goodness is identical. It is just this sort of attempt which the Naturalistic Fallacy is designed to invalidate:

My objections to Naturalism are then, in the first place, that. . . though it gives a reason for no ethical principal, it is a *cause* of the acceptance of false principles—it deludes the mind into accepting ethical principles, which are false; and in this it is contrary to every aim of Ethics. It is easy to see that if we start with a definition of right conduct as conduct conducive to general happiness; then, knowing that right conduct is universally conduct conducive to the good, we very easily arrive at the result that the good is general happiness.[20]

The "*cause* of the acceptance of false principles," the reason why Naturalism "deludes the mind into accepting ethical principles," is, in Moore's eyes, that they each attempt to define, or identify, goodness with one natural property, or set of natural properties, of things. It is not surprising, then, that Moore considers the following reply to be representative of the "naturalist:" " 'This is not an open question: the very meaning of the word (goodness) decides it: no one can think otherwise except through confusion.' "21 It is clear that Moore views "naturalistic ethical theories" as attempting to justify their positions and to cut off debate through a series of verbal definitions of goodness.

But it is just this assumption which characterizes Moore's basic error. If I can put it in a word, Moore fails to see that the "naturalist," such as Hume, is not trying to provide us with a specifically new conception of goodness, or the one "real" definition of goodness, exhaustive and unquestionable. The attempt is rather to provide a new and illuminating organization of pre-existing conceptions and factors, each of them having roots in conduct and utility. Moore believes that the alternative to defining goodness is to conclude that "good is good, and that is the end of the matter."22 But it is precisely this preoccupation with definition and the implications of verbal analysis that characterizes Moore's failure. For he never does recognize the fact that the question of the correct definition of goodness or any other terms of value can only be answered in the light of our answers to the broader and more basic questions concerning the foundations of morality and the methods and principles of organization and interpretation which we ultimately accept. Unless we can begin our ethical discourses with some degree of openness and some sense of the direction in which our values and needs lie, then we cannot very well justify our "definitions" or even what theory of definition we ought to employ.

The lesson is simply that ethical theory, like our moral issues, cannot be isolated and reduced to a mere conceptual framework. Definition, logic, analysis, all have their places in ethical theory. But it is not our logic and definition, but where they lead us that ultimately must stand the test. And we cannot travel well or far if we do not have some sense of priorities and needs, some sense of where we want to go and what we have to work with. Hume, like Mill and Aristotle, is relevant today because he gives intelligent answers to these fundamental questions. But Moore's work, like so much of the work which has followed in his footsteps, has lost its relevance, not because it fails to give intelligent answers to these questions, but because it fails to address itself to them in the first place.

[1]G. E. Moore, "An Autobiography," in *The Philosophy of G. E. Moore,* Edited by Paul Arthur Schilpp, Tudor Publishing Co., 1952.

[2]Ernest Gellner, *Words and Things,* Boston, Beacon Press, 1959, p. 171.

[3]G. E. Moore, "A Defense of Common Sense, in *Philosophical Papers,* London, George Allen & Unwin LTD, 1963, p. 45.

[4]Ernest Gellner, *Words and Things,* Boston, Beacon Press, 1959, p. 91. It is unfortunate that Mr. Gellner does not pursue this very suggestive criticism of Moore in his book.

[5]G. E. Moore, "A Defense of Common Sense," in *Philosophical Papers,* London, George Allen & Unwin LTD, 1963, p. 45.

[6]G. E. Moore, *Principia Ethica,* Cambridge, University Press, 1962, p. 164.

[7]*Ibid.,* p. 162-163.

[8]*Ibid.,* p. 164.

[9]*Ibid.,* p. 161.

[10]Charles Frankel, *The Case for Modern Man,* Boston, Beacon Press, 1966, p. 67.

[11]G. E. Moore, *Principia Ethica,* p. ix.

[12]*Treatise,* p. 269.

[13]*Ibid.,* p. 268.

[14]*Ibid.,* p. 268.

[15]*Ibid.,* p. 270-271.

[16]*Ibid.,* p. 271.

[17]*Principia Ethica,* p. 5.

[18]*Ibid.,* p. XXV.

[19]*Treatise,* p.

[20]*Principia,* p. 20.

[21]*Ibid.,* p. 6.

22